German

Learn German for Beginners: A Simple Guide that Will Help You on Your Language Learning Journey

Contents

Introduction

Hi! We are so glad that you have decided to learn something new in your life. You are about to know everything you need to about the German language. You will soon be able to talk to your German friends or even strangers on German streets.

Your friends, colleagues or family members might have already told you that it is going to be very difficult and that you will need a lot of time—even just to say a few sentences in German. However, guess what? It's time to ERASE those assumptions!

Every new experience can seem complicated or scary at the beginning, but when you take the first few steps, you will see that it isn't that daunting after all. Even if you are a total beginner and don't understand a word in German—it's not an issue. We have the right method to get you going. And for those of you who have some knowledge, but don't know how to use it or need some kind of "push" to finally start speaking the language, then this book is definitely the best option for you.

We have a method that will help you to acquire grammar and vocabulary without annoying memorizing. It is designed for practical, heartfelt and real-life German speaking. Don't worry—you will still learn the important rules throughout the lessons but more conveniently.

This book will not only teach you the rules of German grammar and vocabulary, but it will give you a sense of the soul and music of the German language. You will have a solid beginner's foundation of German, with phrases you can use to navigate social situations and help you to make friends and connections.

Our book is inspiring and vibrant to go through. It shall encourage you to speak and embrace the German language, no matter how new you are to it. It provides English translations for everything too so that you don't become mentally lost, and some explanations that will help you during your learning process.

This is an entertaining, effective and motivating introduction to the German language with ten lessons and various topics that will enable you to train your language skills and use them more efficiently. There is also some cultural information about Germany and interesting dialogues and texts.

Before we dive into the material, let's look at this overview of the lessons first:

1. About Germany

2. Saying "Hi" and Introducing Yourself

3. Talking About the Time, Weather, and Ourselves

4. Education and Work

5. Family and Friends

6. Leisure and Art

7. Food and Drink

8. Clothes and Describing Something

9. Accommodation and Transport

10. Common Questions and Phrases Everyone Needs to Know

Of course, there will be tips and advice throughout the lessons, and you will be able to follow along with everything easily.

Now that you know what you can expect, it is time to start the journey!

Chapter 1 – About Germany

Quick Overview

- The exciting history of the German language

- German, a Germanic language

- The peculiarities of German culture

- Ten ambassadors of the German language

- The great German writers, role models of the German language

Did you know that German is the most widely spoken language in Europe? With more than 100 million speakers worldwide, German occupies the leading position in the European Union, even ahead of English.

If you plan to learn German or live in Germany, it makes sense to get to know both the country's culture and German grammar better. If this applies to you, then you should not forget that language and culture go hand in hand. If you know both the history and the roots of the German language, and how it has changed over time, then you will understand German culture better!

Furthermore, the history of the German language has a few surprises to offer, which you will find out below!

The exciting history of the German language

Around approximately 1,200 years BC, the ancestors of Germanic tribes settled on the peninsula of present-day Denmark. They spoke a language derived from an Indo-European dialect, a mixture of Latin, Celtic, and Sanskrit. One can assume that this dialect forms the origin of the German language. However, there are no traditional documents of this dialect.

This Germanic language also consisted of several dialects: Gothic (extinct since the fourth century), Anglo-Frisian (Dutch and Flemish...) and the Northern Germanic languages (Icelandic, Norwegian...).

At this time, the first sound shift took place. The second took place between the fourth and eighth centuries and led to a change of tone in the area of consonants. The result is called Old High German.

The Grimm Law, named after the German philologist Jacob Grimm, was the first to explain these developments. The word "German" appears for the first time in a document from the year 786.

In the Middle Ages, the German language consisted of several dialects. Nevertheless, there is no standard language during the Middle Ages. At this time, the German language consists of many Germanic dialects. Historians and scientists have discovered texts from this period, mostly of a religious nature. While there are very few German-language texts from the tenth century, from the year 1050, documents can be found in German. These documents are regarded as the first pieces of evidence of Middle High German, the official "forerunner" of modern German. Just like Old High German, there are also several local dialects. Nevertheless, there is a true separation between the two languages. This is mainly because Latin was the literary language from the tenth to the fifteenth century.

The "normal" High German taught today has been driven primarily by the Reformation movement. When Martin Luther translated the Old and New Testaments into German from 1520, the population gradually became German-speaking.

In the nineteenth century, German became an important commercial language. During the Austro-Hungarian empire, German was spoken in Budapest, Prague or Bratislava.

The German dictionary of the Brothers Grimm listed all German words for the first time.

German, a Germanic language

When you learn German, you realize that this language has similarities with other languages, such as English, Persian or Swedish.

Although German is a Germanic language, it belongs to the family of Indo-European languages, the origin of most of the languages spoken in Europe today.

Today, three billion people in the world speak a language derived from this large language family. However, it is known that there was never an Indo-European nation.

In the course of time and conquests, the Indo-European language divided into different branches of language. One branch is the Germanic language, which also includes German. Therefore, there are also similarities between languages that belong to the Germanic languages.

You will notice that the pronunciation is sometimes very similar to English, such as: house – Haus, can – kann, etc.

The phonetics is sometimes very similar too. For example, the emphasis in stressing a particular syllable in the word is the same in both languages.

Also, the conjugation system has similarities with the English language; for example, the division of verbs into strong and weak. These can be compared to the irregular and regular verbs in English. Nevertheless, the German language has specific characteristics.

The declinations are also a peculiarity of the German language. A German teacher will certainly spend many hours teaching a student the different cases. And that is quite normal, as they contribute significantly to the understanding of the German language.

German is also known for its precise expression. The Germans have their own word for everything! For example, "Schadenfreude". This word particularly impresses the non-German world because only they have a word for the joy when others hurt themselves. Of course, they are not happy when someone is seriously hurt.

The peculiarities of German culture

If you want to study or work in Germany or just go on vacation there, you should learn more about the habits of Germans. To perfect your knowledge, you should know the following about German culture:

First and foremost—German cuisine is not just beer and Sauerkraut! Tourists traveling to Germany will get to know a diverse and varied cuisine. For example, the Germans attach great importance to their bread—there are more than 300 different types. The Germans are real bread lovers!

With 1,500 different varieties, the sausage is also a real star in German cuisine. There is sausage in almost every meal.

Of course, you have to eat pretzels when you are in Germany too. They are offered everywhere—in bakeries, stalls in the cities, at festivals, and other events. Did you know that 100,000 pretzels are sold every year at the famous Munich Oktoberfest?

The inhabitants of Germany and their everyday life also represent German culture.

For many Germans, the topics of family and school/education are extremely important. The children are the center of life in German families. Strangers who come to Germany to work might quickly get the impression that German families are all about the children. In Germany the children are freer, are allowed to develop freely, and have fewer rules imposed on them.

When it comes to working in Germany, work experience is more important than a diploma. The Germans speak candidly at work—they say what they think and are very direct.

In addition, the Germans place more value on following rules.

Even though these observations are very clichéd, they still contain a grain of truth!

Ten ambassadors of the German language

Albert Einstein: physicist and inventor of the theory of relativity. Einstein was a German citizen who was born on March 14, 1879 in Ulm, Baden-Württemberg—"was" because he left Nazi Germany in 1933 after Hitler came to power in order to be initially stateless, then went on to accept Swiss citizenship, and finally, until his death, American-Swiss citizenship (in Princeton, 1955).

Martin Luther: the author of Protestantism and the Reformation movement. He translated the Lutheran Bible.

Anne Frank: a symbol of the atrocities of the Nazi regime and the Second World War. She was killed at the age of fifteen during the Holocaust and is the author of *The Diary of Anne Frank*, which she wrote while hiding from the Nazis. The novel is now a classic of world literature.

Other persons who played or play an important role in Germany:

Ludwig van Beethoven, composer.

Immanuel Kant, philosopher.

Johann Wolfgang von Goethe, a writer whose name often serves as a synonym for the German language.

Karl May, writer.

Claudia Schiffer, top model.

Boris Becker, tennis legend.

Karl Lagerfeld, fashion designer.

Horst Tappert, the famous inspector Derrick.

The great German writers, role models of the German language

German literature plays a central role in the circles of world literature. If you have not read something from a German author during your schooling or study period, it is far from too late. The following is a small reading list with works by great German writers:

Johann Wolfgang von Goethe. His name has become synonymous with the German language; after all, one often speaks of the "language of Goethe"! He has written the famous poem "Prometheus", The play *Faust*, and the novel *Elective Affinities*.

Patrick Süskind. The author of *Perfume*.

To complete your knowledge of German literature, you should also read the following authors:

The Brothers Grimm

Thomas Mann

Stefan Zweig

Now you are more familiar with German culture and the history of the language. It is always good to have some basic knowledge so that you feel closer to the country.

We can now move on to the next chapter, where you will finally get the chance to learn the basics of the language.

Chapter 2 – Saying "Hi" and Introducing Yourself

Quick Overview

- Vocabulary
- Forming the plural
- Greeting someone and saying goodbye
- Introducing yourself
- Saying thank you and please
- Verbs: sein (to be), haben (to have), kommen (to come), heißen (to be called), wohnen (to live).
- Word order

Before we start with the important phrases in German used to greet someone, it is important to know some vocabulary first:

der Tag – Day

der Morgen – Morning

der Vormittag (10:00 – 12:00) – forenoon

der Mittag (12:00 – 14:00) – noon

der Nachmittag (14:00 – 18:00) – afternoon

der Abend (18:00 – 21:00) – evening

die Nacht – night

die Woche – week

der Monat – the month

das Jahr – the year

If you want to say "yesterday", you will say: gestern

If you want to say "today", you will say: heute

If you want to say "tomorrow", you will say: morgen

What do you notice when you look at these words? What type of words are they? Right! Nouns. In German, the first letter of the noun is always a capital letter. Another thing about nouns is that they always have an article "der, die, or das". We will talk about nouns and articles as we go because there are many of them and there is no use of learning the whole list at once.

Another characteristic of nouns is that they can be in the plural form as well. It is crucial for you to know how the plural is formed before we move on.

Most nouns have two forms:

Singular: The singular indicates that the corresponding noun exists only once.

Here is an example:

Es dauert eine **Woche**. – It lasts one week.

The important word is "die Woche" (week), which is in the singular.

Plural: The plural indicates that the corresponding noun exists several times.

Es dauert zwei Woche**n**. – It lasts two weeks.

As you can see, now the word "Woche" has an "n" at the end in the plural.

In the plural form, no general rule can be determined. However, most nouns form their plural form with "(e)n" or "e". Some form an umlaut in the plural formation (ä / ö / ü).

All nouns in the plural have the plural article "die".

We distinguish between the following **plural forms**:

Masculine and neutral nouns that end in -er, -en, -el, -chen, -lein have no plural ending. Masculine nouns often get an umlaut.

das Jahr – die Jahre (year), der Monat – die Monate (month), der Apfel – die Äpfel (apple)

das Mädchen – die Mädchen (girl), der Garten – die Gärten (garden), der Vater – die Väter (father)

das Männlein – die Männlein (little man), das Zeichen – die Zeichen (sign), der Vogel – die Vögel (bird)

Most masculine and neutral nouns form their plural form with -e. The masculine nouns often have an umlaut, feminine nouns always.

der Fall – die Fälle (case), das Boot – die Boote (boat), die Kuh – die Kühe (cow)

der Tag – die Tage (day), das Gedicht – die Gedichte (poem), die Maus – die Mäuse (mouse)

der Tisch – die Tische (table), das Telefon – die Telefone (phone), die Nacht – die Nächte (night).

All masculine nouns of n-declination, most feminine nouns, many foreign words, and some neutral nouns form their plural form with - (e)n. The plural form in this group is almost always formed without umlaut.

der Junge – die Jungen (boy), das Auge – die Augen (eye), die Frage – die Fragen (question)

der Löwe – die Löwen (lion), das Bett – die Betten (bed), die Idee – die Ideen (idea) der Student – die Studenten (student), das Ohr – die Ohren (ear), die Straße – die Straßen (street).

Most neutral nouns and some masculine nouns form their plural form with the ending -er. In this group most nouns with the self-sounds a, o or u form an umlaut.

das Buch – die Bücher (book), das Land – die Länder (land), das Wort – die Wörter (word)

das Haus – die Häuser (house), der Mann – die Männer (man), der Wald – die Wälder (forest)

das Bild – die Bilder (photo), das Kind – die Kinder (child), das Licht – die Lichter (light).

Nouns with the suffixes a, i, o or u, abbreviations and foreign words form their plural form with -s.

das Foto – die Fotos (photo), das Kino – die Kinos (cinema), das Taxi – die Taxis(cab)

das Sofa – die Sofas (couch), die Oma – die Omas (grandma), der Opa – die Opas (grandpa)

der PC – die PCs (PC), das Team – die Teams (team).

Nouns ending in -nis and -in double their consonants.

das Ereignis – die Ereignisse (event), das Ergebnis – die Ergebnisse (result)

die Ärztin – die Ärztinnen (doctor-female), die Lehrerin – die Lehrerinnen (teacher-female).

Some nouns are only used in the singular or only in the plural. The most important ones are listed here:

Only Singular

das Alter – the age

der Ärger – the anger

der Frieden – the peace

die Geduld – the patience

die Hitze – the heat

der Lärm – the noise

das Geld – the money

das Glück – the luck

die Kälte – the cold

Only Plural

die Einkünfte – the groceries

die Eltern – the parents

die Ferien – the holidays

die Gebrüder – the brothers

die Kosten – the prices

die Geschwister – the siblings

die Lebensmittel – foods

You now know the basics when it comes to the plural form. We can now continue. One of the first things you need to do when you see a stranger you want to talk to, or a friend or someone you know, is greet them.

Greeting someone

In Germany, when you see someone whom you need to talk to in a formal way, you will say:

Good Morning! – Guten Morgen!

Good evening! – Guten Abend!

Good day! – Guten Tag!

When you want to be less formal, use these expressions:

Hello! –Hallo!

Hey! – Hey!

Good night! – Gute Nacht!

Good day! – Grüß Gott! (in Southern Germany and Austria)

Nice to see you/you. – Schön Sie/dich zu sehen.

Don't get confused by "you" written two times. It is just because in German, "Sie" (with "S" written big) is a formal way of saying "you". We use it when talking to strangers, authorities, older people, our boss at work, and so on.

Let's see how you would say goodbye to someone:

Saying goodbye

Goodbye! – Auf Wiedersehen!

Bye for now! – Bis bald!

Good night! – Gute Nacht!

Goodbye! – Ciao! (informal)

Goodbye! – Tschüss! (informal)

Germans will often shorten everything and just say this to greet you:

Morgen! – Morning

Tag! – Day!

Abend! – Evening!

You will probably need the words yes, no or maybe at some point. This is how you say them:

Yes – Ja

No – Nein

Maybe – Vielleicht

Kommst du morgen? – Are you coming tomorrow?

Ja/Nein/Vielleicht. – Yes/No/Maybe.

Now it is time to introduce yourself and engage in small talk.

Introducing yourself/asking someone about them

Let's say that you are coming across a stranger whom you want to meet and get to know. Maybe you just landed in Germany and you want to ask for some basic information. You will first greet this person and introduce yourself. It is around 10 o'clock in the morning.

Good morning! – Guten Morgen!

I am Anna – Ich bin Anna.

I'm visiting Germany for the first time. – Ich besuche Deutschland zum ersten Mal.

What's your name? – Wie heißen Sie (formal) / Wie heißt du (informal)?

My name is Mark – Mein Name ist Mark.

I am 25 years old – Ich bin 18 Jahre alt.

How old are you? – Wie alt bist du? (informal) / Wie alt sind Sie? (formal)

I am from Germany. – Ich komme aus Deutschland.

Where are you from? – Woher kommen Sie/Woher kommst du?

Are you coming from...? – Kommen Sie aus…/Kommst du aus?

Yes, I'm from ... – Ja, ich komme aus…

Are you from…? – Kommst du aus/Kommen Sie aus?

No. I'm from… – Nein, ich komme aus…

I am visiting as a tourist – Ich bin hier als Tourist.

I have a job interview – Ich habe ein Bewerbungsgespräch.

If you are already in the middle of a conversation where you talk about some personal information, then you will need some more phrases:

I live in Munich – Ich lebe in München.

I live alone – Ich lebe alleine.

I live with my parents and two sisters – Ich lebe mit meinen Eltern und zwei Schwestern.

I live in a house – Ich wohne in einem Haus.

I live in an apartment – Ich wohne in einer Wohnung.

Where do you live? – Wo wohnen Sie? / Wo wohnst du?

I live in an apartment with my roommate. – Ich wohne in einem Apartment mit meinem Zimmergenossen.

I come from Berlin, but I am studying in Frankfurt. – Ich komme aus Berlin, aber ich studiere in Frankfurt.

At the moment I live with my boyfriend. We are both students – Zurzeit wohne ich mit meinem Freund zusammen. Wir beide sind Studenten.

I live together with my girlfriend. Her name is Paula and we have only been here for a year – Ich wohne zusammen mit meiner Freundin. Ihr Name ist Paula und wir sind erst seit einem Jahr hier.

My husband got a job in Germany. That is why I decided to come with him and I'm looking for a job right now – Mein Mann hat in Deutschland einen Job bekommen. Deswegen habe ich entschieden, mit ihm zu kommen und ich bin gerade auch auf der Suche nach einem Job.

I live in a small apartment together with my wife – Ich wohne in einer kleinen Wohnung mit meiner Frau zusammen.

Since I am still in school, I live with my parents – Da ich immer noch zur Schule gehe, wohne ich bei meinen Eltern.

I live together with my friends. We rent a shared flat – Ich wohne zusammen mit meinen Freunden. Wir haben eine WG gemietet.

At the moment I live with relatives. It is easier for me – Zurzeit lebe ich mit Verwandten zusammen. Es ist einfacher so für mich.

Do you live on your own or with someone? – Lebst du allein oder mit jemandem zusammen?

I live on my own – Ich lebe allein

I have a roommate and we live together – Ich habe einen Mitbewohner / eine Mitbewohnerin mit der ich zusammen wohne.

I have two/ three/more roommates/roommates – Ich habe zwei/drei/mehr Mitbewohner / Mitbewohnerinnen.

When talking about where you come from, you can easily answer with some simple phrases or even talk a little deeper about your origin and relatives. You can ask your conversation partner the same questions for small talk.

Where are you from? – Woher kommst du?

Where does your family come from? – Woher kommt deine Familie?

Where does your father/mother come from? – Woher kommt dein Vater/deine Mutter?

I am from Chicago – Ich bin aus Chicago.

What part of Chicago do you come from? – Aus welchem Teil von Chicago kommst du?

Where exactly is that? – Wo genau befindet sich das?

I was there once. It was really nice – Ich war mal dort. Es war wirklich schön.

I was never there, but I would like to visit sometime – Ich war noch nie dort, aber ich würde es gerne besuchen.

In which city do you live? – In welcher Stadt wohnst du?

I live in London – Ich wohne in London.

I am originally from Spain, but I live now in Germany – Ich komme ursprünglich aus Spanien, aber jetzt lebe ich in Deutschland.

I was born in Germany but grew up in England – Ich bin in Deutschland geboren, aber aufgewachsen bin ich in England.

My family was in Switzerland during the war. Then we came back to Germany. We have been living here for a long time – Meine Familie war während des Kriegs in der Schweiz. Danach sind wir wieder nach Deutschland gekommen. Wir leben hier schon lange.

My grandparents are from Germany. My father wanted us to come here as well – Meine Großeltern sind aus Deutschland. Mein Vater wollte, dass wir auch hierher kommen.

What brings you to Germany? – Was bringt dich nach Deutschland?

I am on holiday here. I really like it – Ich mache hier nur Urlaub. Ich mage es hier sehr.

I am on business trip and I want to use this opportunity to look around a bit – Ich bin auf Geschätsreise und nutze die Gelegenheit mich auch ein bisschen umzusehen.

I have been living here for two years – Ich lebe hier schon seit zwei Jahren.

I work here as a nurse – Ich arbeite hier als Krankenschwester.

I am studying in Berlin and that is why I am here – Ich studiere in Berlin und deswegen bin ich hier.

I always wanted to live abroad. That was my dream. So I decided to come here and look for a job. Now I am here working in a great company – Ich wollte schon immer im Ausland leben. Das war mein Traum. So habe ich mich entschieden hierher zu kommen und nach einem Job zu suchen. Jetzt bin ich hier und arbeite in einer großartigen Firma.

How long are you here? – Wie lange bist du den schon hier?

I have just moved here – Ich bin gerade erst hierher gezogen.

I have been living here for a few months. That is why my German is not that good yet – Ich lebe hier seit ein paar Monaten. Deswegen ist mein Deutsch noch nicht so gut.

I have been living here for a year and I like it very much – Ich lebe hier schon ein Jahr und mit gefällt es sehr gut.

I am here for a little over two years – Ein bisschen länger als zwei Jahre bin ich hier.

How long do you want to stay? What are your plans? – Wie lange willst du bleiben? Was für Pläne hast du?

I want to stay here until August. I would like to visit and see some more – Ich will bis August hier bleiben. Ich möchte noch einiges besuchen und sehen.

A few months until I have holidays. Then I go back to Spain. But I will come back to Germany to work – Ein paar Monate bis ich Ferien habe. Dann gehe ich wieder nach Spanien zurück. Ich werde aber wieder nach Deutschland kommen, um zu arbeiten.

I have to stay one more year until my studies are over. I have some more exams. After that I plan to look for a job in Germany. I want to stay here forever – Ich muss noch ein Jahr bleiben, bis mein Studium zu Ende ist. Ich habe noch einige Prüfungen. Danach plane ich in Deutschland nach einem Job zu suchen. Ich möchte hier für immer bleiben.

I am not sure. I have not planned anything yet – Ich bin nicht sicher. Ich habe noch nichts geplant.

Do you like it here? – Magst du es hier?

Yes, I love it! I like the city, the people, the way they live here. Everything is great – Ja, ich liebe es! Ich mag die Stadt, die Menschen, die Art, wie man hier lebt. Einfach alles ist super.

I really like it. It is different than my homeland. Everything is much better here – Ich mag es sehr. Es ist anders als mein Heimatland. Hier ist alles viel besser.

It is alright so far – Bis jetzt ist es in Ordnung.

What do you like here the most? – Was gefällt dir hier besonders?

I like a lot here, but most of all I like the food. I love the German specialties and the tradition – Ich mag sehr vieles hier, doch am meisten mag ich das Essen. Ich liebe die deutschen Spezialitäten und die Tradition.

The weather here is very nice. It is just perfect for everything – Das Wetter hier ist sehr schön. Es ist einfach perfekt für alles.

The people are very friendly and willing to help. I like how organized everyone is and how everything works in the city – Die Leute sind hier sehr freundlich und bereit zu helfen. Ich mag wie organisiert alle sind und die Art wie alles in der Stadt funktioniert.

What are you doing here? – Was machst du so hier?

My everyday life is nothing special. I get up, go to school and then I usually have to study or go eat with my friends – Mein Alltag ist nichts besonderes. Ich stehe auf, gehe zur Schule und danach muss ich meistens lernen oder ich gehe mit meinen Freunden etwas essen.

I go to work in the morning. After that I like to watch a movie in my flat, or go for a walk. This relaxes me a lot. I also like to go shopping – Ich gehe morgens zur Arbeit. Danach mag ich es, einen Film in meiner Wohnung anzuschauen, oder ich mache einen Spaziergang. Dies entspannt mich sehr. Ich mag es aber auch einkaufen zu gehen.

Why are you in Germany? – Warum bist du in Deutschland?

What are you doing in Germany? – Was machst du in Deutschland?

Because I want to work/study here – Weil ich hier arbeiten/studieren möchte.

I am just visiting as a tourist. I like to travel a lot and Germany was one of my wishes for a long time – Ich bin nur als Tourist hier. Ich mag es zu reisen und Deutschland warschon lange mein Wunsch.

What do you think about this place? – Wie fühlst du über diesen Ort?

It is great. I really like the people and the atmosphere – Es ist ausgezeichnet. Ich mag die Menschen und die Atmosphäre.

Good. I like the city, but the weather is bad – Gut. Ich finde die Stadt schön, aber ich mag das Wetter nicht.

How long have you been here? – Wie lange bist du schon hier?

I have been here for three days – Ich bin hier schon seit drei Tagen.

Whom are you traveling with? – Mit wem reist du?

I am traveling with my sister/husband/wife... – Ich reise mit meiner Schwester/Mann/Frau...

Would you like to go out? – Möchtest du mit mir ausgehen?

Of course! When do we meet? – Natürlich! Wann treffen wir uns?

If you get more comfortable with the person, you can start talking about what you like and what not:

I like animals. Especially cats. They really fascinate me a lot. I have three cats and I want to have a lot more – Ich mag Tiere. Besonders Katzen. Sie faszinieren mich wirklich sehr. Ich habe drei Katzen und möchte noch viel mehr haben.

I like nature. Nature relaxes and calms me. I just like lying in a meadow and looking into the blue sky. It works wonders – Ich mag die Natur. Die Natur entspannt und beruhigt mich. Ich mag es einfach nur auf einer Wiese zu liegen und in den blauen Himmel zu schauen. Das wirkt bei mir sehr gut.

I like sports. I have always been a sporty person. I used to practice tennis and now I just like to go jogging or swimming. I am always active because that is how I feel best – Ich mag Sport. Ich war schon immer ein sportlicher Mensch. Früher habe ich Tennis trainiert und jetzt mag ich es, einfach joggen zu gehen oder zu schwimmen. Ich bin immer aktiv, denn so fühle ich mich am besten.

I like spending time with my family. We often do a picnic over the weekend. That connects us even more – Ich mag es, mit meiner Familie die Zeit zu verbringen. Wir machen oft am Wochenende ein Picknik. Das verbindet uns noch mehr.

I love to spend time with my friends. We often go to a movie or we go to a concert. Sometimes we just go dancing in a club – Ich liebe es mit meinen Freunden Zeit zu verbringen. Wir gehen oft einen Film anschauen oder wir gehen auf ein Konzert. Manchmal gehen wir einfach nur in einem Club tanzen.

Did you go to the concert last night? – Warst du beim Konzert letzte Nacht?

I like the band… – Ich mag die Band …

Yes, I was at the concert. It was just awesome. Who were you with? – Ja, ich war beim Konzert. Es war einfach genial. Mit wem warst du dort?

I was there with my girlfriend. She persuaded me, and in the end we had a lot of fun – Ich war da mit meiner Freundin. Sie hat mich überredet, und am Ende hatten wir viel Spaß.

I have a dog called Leo – Ich habe einen Hund der Leo heißt.

Do you own a pet? – Hast du ein Haustier?

No, I don't. But I had a cat earlier – Nein, das habe ich nicht. Ich hatte aber früher eine Katze.

If you want to stay in touch with the person you just talked to, then you could also use the following phrases.

Ask for contact details – Nach Kontaktdaten fragen

If you were talking to someone your age or with someone whom you want to hang out with, then you could say:

Hey, I really liked our conversation. We should maybe meet again. What do you think? – Hey, ich fand unser Gespräch wirklich toll. Wir sollten uns vielleicht mal wieder treffen. Was meinst du?

Yes, gladly. I also found it very nice. Let's exchange numbers – Ja, gerne. Ich fand es auch sehr nett. Lass uns Nummern austauschen.

Do you have a phone number? – Hast du eine Telefonnummer?

What is your phone number? – Wie ist deine Telefonnummer?

If you are exchanging contacts with someone important like your new boss or someone whom you need to talk to formally, then you can exchange e-mail addresses:

What is your email address? – Wie ist deine E-mail-Adresse?

What is your address? – Wie ist deine Adresse?

Could I take your phone number? – Kann ich deine Telefonnummer haben?

Could I take your email address? – Kann ich deine E-mail-Adresse haben?

You can also ask for social media:

Do you have facebook? – Hast du vielleicht Facebook?

Do you use Skype? What is your name on there? – Benutzt du Skype? Wie lautet dein Name dort?

What is your username? – Was ist dein Benutzername?

Sometimes you will be in a situation where you will need to introduce someone else to your friends or someone important. Here is how to do it:

Do you know Maria? – Kennst du Maria?

This is Maria, my wife – Dies ist Maria, meine Ehefrau.

This is my husband – Das ist mein Ehemann.

This is my son/daughter/friend – Das ist mein Sohn/Tochter/Freund/in.

I am sorry, what is your name again? – Entschuldigung, wie ist dein Name?

Did you already meet each other? – Habt ihr euch schon kennengelernt?

Nice to meet you – Schön, dich kennenzulernen

Pleased to meet you – Freut mich sehr, dich kennenzulernen

How do you know each other? – Wie habt ihr euch kennengelernt?

We work in the same company. We met only a few months ago – Wir arbeiten in derselben Firma. Wir haben uns erst vor einigen Monaten kennengelernt.

We worked together in the same company a couple of years ago. Since then we are best friends – Wir haben vor ein paar Jahren zusammen in der gleichen Firma gearbeitet. Seitdem sind wir beste Freunde.

We went to the same school. We were best friends back then, but he/she moved after that. – Wir gingen auf die gleiche Schule. Damals waren wir beste Freunde, doch sie/er ist danach umgezogen.

We study together – Wir studieren zusammen.

We studied together. We often learned together and drank coffee – Wir haben zusammen studiert. Oft haben wir zusammen gelernt und Kaffee getrunken.

These were some of the most important phrases for when you talk to someone new or someone you know a little. Now on to how to say please and thank you.

Please and thank you – Bitte und Danke

Bitte – please

This word is often used when talking politely.

Kannst du mir bitte den Stift geben? – Can you please give me the pen?

The word "bitte" is often put in the middle of the sentence.

If you want to answer to "bitte", say:

Gerne – you are welcome

Bitte sehr – here you are

Danke – thank you

Danke sehr or Danke schön– thank you or thank you very much

Entschuldigung – sorry

Examples:

(Entschuldigung) Wie spät ist es, bitte? – (Sorry) What time is it, please?

Es ist 10 Uhr. Danke sehr – It is 10 o'clock. Thank you very much.

Wie geht es dir/ Ihnen? – How are you?

Danke gut – Good, thank you.

Darf ich bitte einen Stift haben? – Can I please have a pen?

Danke für den Stift – Thank you for the pen.

Kann ich bitte ein Glas Wasser haben? – Can I have a cup of water, please?

Einen Kaffe, bitte – One coffee, please.

Important verbs

Sein – to be (irregular verb)

Haben – to have (irregular for the second and third person singular: du, er, sie, es)

Heißen – to be called/be named

Kommen – to come

Wohnen – to live

These verbs are important because we use them to talk about ourselves or to ask others about them, their name, where they come from, and so on. Of course, we cannot use the infinitive of the verbs in sentences.

SEIN

We use this verb to say who we are, where we come from, how we are, and to talk about our characteristics. We can use it to describe someone else:

Er ist Arzt – He is a doctor. (Occupation)

Er ist aus München – He is from Munich. (Ancestry)

Er ist in Spanien – He is in Spain. (Place)

Das ist Frau Schmidt – This is Ms. Schmidt (sein, to be + Nomen, noun).

Sie ist sehr interessant. – She is very interesting (sein, to be + Adjektiv, adjective).

Conjugation

Ich **bin** – I am

Du **bist** – You are

Er/Sie/Es **ist** – He/She/It is

Wir **sind** – We are

Ihr **seid** – You are

Sie **sind** – They are

Examples:

Ich <u>bin</u> Anna – I am Anna.

Du <u>bist</u> David – You are David.

Wir <u>sind</u> aus Spanien – We are from Spain.

Sie <u>sind</u> aus Amerika – They are from America.

HABEN

We use "haben" for belongings. When we want to say that we have a car, a brother, a job, a house, brown hair, blue eyes, a dress, etc., then we use this verb.

Ich habe eine Katze – I have a cat.

Er hat blaue Augen – He has blue eyes.

Sie hat einen Bruder – She has a brother.

Wir haben viel zu tun – We have much to do.

Ihr habt Hausaufgaben – You have homework.

Conjugation

Ich **habe** – I have

Du **hast** – You have

Er, sie, es **hat** – He, she, it has

Wir **haben** – We have

Ihr **habt** – You have

Sie **haben** – They have

HEIßEN

We use the verb "heißen" to say our or the name of someone else. We could translate it as "I am" or "My name is".

Ich heiße David – I am David. My name is David.

Sie heißt Anna – She is Anna. Her name is Anna.

Wie heißt du? – What is your name?

Heißen, kommen, wohnen and the majority of German verbs are regular verbs that we conjugate by adding certain endings to the verb stem for each person in singular and plural.

Let's see the endings for each person:

Ich (-e)

Du (-st)

Er/Sie/Es (-t)

Wir (-en)

Ihr (-t)

Sie (-en)

But we can't add those endings to the infinitive. We need to add them to the verb stem. And this applies to all the regular verbs.

For example, we have the verb "heißen". We get the verb stem by removing the ending (-en). Then we are just left with "heiß" and this is the verb stem that we need.

Ich heiß**e**

Du heis**st (ss=ß)**

Er, Sie, Es heiß**t**

Wir heiß**en**

Ihr heiß**t**

Sie heiß**en**

KOMMEN

"Kommen" is another regular verb that we conjugate just like the previous verb "heißen". This verb is used when saying the country, city or place that someone comes from or can be used like the English verb "to come".

Ich komme aus Berlin – I come from Berlin.

Sara kommt morgen nach Hause – Sara comes home tomorrow.

Frank kommt zur Party – Frank comes to the party.

Wir kommen aus Spanien – We come from Spain.

Woher kommt sie? – Where is she from?

Conjugation

Ich komm**e**

Du komm**st**

Er, Sie, Es komm**t**

Wir komm**en**

Ihr komm**t**

Sie komm**en**

As you can see, the endings are the same, just like the endings for the previous verb. These endings are the same for all the regular verbs.

You can try it for yourself and conjugate the verb "wohnen" before we do it in the following section. Just try to do it in your head and check your results.

WOHNEN

This verb is used for stating where someone lives when it comes to the type of building, i.e., a house, an apartment, etc., or is used to say whom someone lives with.

Ich wohne in einer Wohnung – I live in an apartment.

Sie wohnt in einem Haus – She lives in a house.

Wir wohnen in einem Zimmer – We live in a room.

Du wohnst mit deiner Schwester – You live with your sister.

Er wohnt dort seit drei Jahren – He has been living there for three years.

Wo wohnst du? – Where do you live?

Conjugation

Ich wohn**e**

Du wohn**st**

Er, Sie, Es wohn**t**

Wir wohn**en**

Ihr wohn**t**

Sie wohn**en**

Now that you know about verbs let's look at **WORD ORDER** in a sentence.

We will just cover the word order in the main clause. A sentence consists of the **subject** (person or thing performing the activity), **predicate** (conjugated verb), and possibly other clauses.

In a main clause (with a dot at the end) the predicate is in second place.

I – II – III

Ich – gehe – heute – ins Kino.

I go today to the cinema. (literal translation)

Unser – Vater – spielt – gern – Tennis.

Our father likes playing tennis.

Natalie – schreibt – nicht – gern.

Natalie does not like to write.

If another clause comes first in a main clause, the subject comes immediately after the predicate.

Heute – gehe – ich – ins Kino.

Today I go to the cinema.

As you can see, the subject "ich" (I) came right after the verb "gehe".

Questions

Question without a question word: predicate comes in the first place, then comes the subject.

I – II – III

Gehst – du – heute – ins Kino?

Are you going to the cinema today?

Gibt – es – etwas über Design?

Is there something about design?

On such a decision question, one answers "yes" or "no."

Supplementary question – with question word: in the first place is the question word, in the second place the predicate, then comes the subject.

I – II – III

Wohin – gehst – du – heute?

Where are you going today?

Wie – ist – dein – Name?

What is your name?

Wo – ist – die – Ausstellung?

Where is the exhibition?

Wohin – gehst – du – heute?

Where are you going today?

Question words

Question words are very important and make the forming of the question easier. They begin with the letter "w-".

Let's take a look at them:

Wer? – Who?

Wer ist das? – Who is that?

Was? – What?

Was möchtest du essen? – What do you want to eat?

Was machen wir heute? – What are we doing today?

Wessen? – Whose?

Wessen Hund ist das? – Whose dog is this?

Wem? – Whom?

Wem soll ich helfen? – Whom should I help?

Wen? – Who?

Wen besuchen wir heute? – Whom are we visiting today?

Warum? – Why?

Warum bist du traurig? – Why are you sad?

Wann? – When?

Wann kommst du zu uns? – When are you coming to us?

Wo? – Where?

Wo wohnst du? – Where do you live?

Wohin? – To where?

Wohin fahrt ihr im Urlaub? – Where are you driving to on vacation?

Woher? – From where?

Woher kommst du? – Where are you from?

These were the question words, and now we need to focus on another important part of each sentence: the object.

Order of the objects in the sentence

If two objects occur as nouns in the sentence, the dative object comes before the accusative object. You can see this from the following example:

Ich gebe **meinem Freund** das Buch – (meinem Freund – to my friend: dative); (das Buch – the book: accusative).

I give the book to my friend. (We are used to another order in English.)

The object as a personal pronoun is always in front of the object as a noun.

Ich gebe **ihm** das Buch. (The dative of the personal pronoun comes before the object in the accusative.)

I give him the book.

Ich gebe es **ihm**. (The object as a personal pronoun "es" comes before the object as a noun.)

I give it to him.

If two objects occur as personal pronouns in the sentence, the accusative object stands in front of the dative object.

Ich gebe **meinem Freund** das Buch.

I give the book to my friend.

Ich gebe es **ihm**. (Accusative stands before dative.)

I give it to him.

Negation "nicht" (not)

The negation "nicht" is used to deny the whole sentence or part of a sentence.

When negating the whole sentence, we put "nicht" at the end of the sentence, but before the second verb.

Ich liebe dich **nicht**.

I do not love you.

Leider kann ich **nicht** schwimmen. (Können – kann = first verb; schwimmen = second verb.)

Unfortunately, I cannot swim.

When negating part of a sentence, "nicht" comes before the negated part of the sentence.

Ich will jetzt **nicht** schwimmen (sondern in einer Stunde).

I do not want to swim now (but in an hour).

Sie geht **nicht** mit Mario (sondern mit Peter).

She does not go with Mario (but with Peter).

We will stop here when it comes to the word order in a sentence and in questions. We will discuss the other options as we go. We hope that you learned a lot from our first lesson and that you are ready to continue!

Chapter 3 – Talking About the Time, Weather and Ourselves

Quick Overview

- Vocabulary
- The time
- The date and months
- The definite articles: der, die, das.
- The indefinite articles: ein, eine, ein

We will now learn colors, numbers, the time, weather, and some other necessary things so that we can move on to the "serious" stuff.

Vocabulary

Colors – Farben

Red – Rot

Blue – Blau

Yellow – Gelb

White – Weiß

Black – Schwarz

Green – Grün

Orange – Orange

Purple – Violett

Gray – Grau

Numbers – die Zahlen

Zero – Null

One – Eins

Two – Zwei

Three – Drei

Four – Vier

Five – Fünf

Six – Sechs

Seven – Sieben

Eight – Acht

Nine – Neun

Ten – Zehn

Eleven – Elf

Twelve – Zwölf

Thirteen – Dreizehn

Fourteen – Vierzehn

Fifteen – Fünfzehn

Sixteen – Sechzehn

Seventeen – Siebzehn

Eighteen – Achtzehn

Nineteen – Neunzehn

Twenty – Zwanzig

Twenty-one – Einundzwanzig

Twenty-two – Zweiundzwanzig

Twenty-three – Dreiundzwanzig

Twenty-four – Vierundzwanzig

Twenty-five – Fünfundzwanzig

Twenty-six – Sechsundzwanzig

Twenty-seven – Siebenundzwanzig

Twenty-eight – Achtundzwanzig

Twenty-nine – Neunundzwanzig

Thirty – Dreißig

Forty – Vierzig

Fifty – Fünfzig

Sixty – Sechszig

Seventy – Siebzig

Eighty – Achtzig

Ninety – Neunzig

One Hundred – Hundert

Two Hundred – Zweihundert

Thousand – Tausend

Two Thousand – Zweitausend

Ten Thousand – Zehntausend

Months – Monate

January – Januar

February – Februar

March – März

April – April

May – Mai

June – Juni

July – Juli

August – August

September – September

October – Oktober

November – November

December – Dezember

Seasons – Jahreszeiten

Spring – Frühling

Summer – Sommer

Autumn/Fall – Herbst

Winter – Winter

The time – Die Uhrzeit

The German language has two options when asking for the time:

What time is it? – Wieviel Uhr ist es?

What time is it? – Wie spät ist es?

As in many other European languages, there are two ways to say the time in German: an official one (at the train station or the airport) or an unofficial option. This unofficial option is mostly used in private conversations or when the exact time is not so important.

The official time

The official time is easy to understand and learn.

For 22:10 clock, say: 22 Uhr 10

For 6:18 clock, say: 6 Uhr 18

The official time is 24 hours. First, say the hours, then the word "Uhr", and then the minutes.

This works for other units. For example, if we talk about 7.50 meters, we say "sieben Meter fünfzig". It is the same with amounts of money: 3.99 euros are "drei Euro neunundneunzig."

The unofficial time

The unofficial time is more difficult but not impossible to understand.

For the unofficial time, we only use 12 hours.

To say more precisely what time of the day it is, say "am Morgen" (in the morning), "am Vormittag" (before noon) "am Mittag" (at noon), "am Nachmittag" (in the afternoon), "am Abend"(in the evening) or "in der Nacht" (at Night).

Let's look at some examples to explain the unofficial time.

13:05 clock:

Unofficially say: fünf NACH eins (am Mittag). (five after one – at noon)

When still in the first half hour, say how many minutes AFTER the last full hour. Use the preposition NACH.

13:15:

Unofficially say: VIERTEL NACH eins (quarter after one). One could also say "fünfzehn nach eins."

13:20:

Unofficially say: zwanzig NACH eins.

When it is 13:30, it is in the middle of 13 and 14 o'clock.

Then use the word HALB, and say: halb zwei.

After the middle of 13 and 14 o'clock, we orient the next hour, 14 o'clock. Use the preposition VOR. Then say how many minutes are left until 14 or 2 o'clock.

13:35:

Unofficially say: 25 VOR zwei.

13:45:

The unofficial variant is: VIERTEL VOR zwei..

13:50 clock:

Unofficially say: zehn VOR zwei.

There is another unofficial variant for minutes 25 and 35. Here is another way to express the time.

Examples:

8:25 – fünf vor halb neun

8:30 – halb neun

8:35 – fünf nach halb neun

Here we orient ourselves at half an hour and say how many minutes we have BEFORE or AFTER "halb".

If we talk about the time in a sentence, we use the preposition "um" (at).

Wann kommst du? – When are you coming?

Ich komme um drei Uhr – I come at three o'clock.

Wann kommt der Bus? – When does the bus arrive?

Um halb sechs – At half six.

Um wieviel Uhr ist das Konzert? – What time is the concert?

Um viertel vor acht – At a quarter to eight.

When it comes to the months, we use the preposition "im" (in).

Example

Wann ist dein Termin? – When is your appointment?

im Januar, im Februar, im März, im April... – in January, in February, in March, in April.

The adjectives "last", "this" or "next" are used, and we say those in the Accusative:

letzten Januar/letzten Februar/letzten März... – last January/last February/last March

diesen April/diesen Mai/diesen Juni... – this April/this May/ this June

nächsten Juli/nächsten August/nächsten September... – next July/next August/next September

Example:

Die Prüfung war letzten Februar –The exam was last February.

Ich gehe nach Deutschland diesen September – I am going to Germany this September.

Du musst dich nächsten Juli bewerben – You have to sign up next July.

When it comes to the exact date, we use the preposition "am" (on).

am 3. Oktober 1995 – on the 3. October 1995.

am 9.3.2012 – on the 9.3.2012.

vom 7. bis zum 15. Juni – from the 7. to the 15. June.

vor dem 13. April – before the 13. April.

ab (dem) 8. September – from the 8. September.

Der, Die, Das

Before we move on, there are some rules when it comes to German articles. There are three of them: "der, die, das".

As in many other languages, in German, the nouns are distinguished according to gender. Each noun also has a companion, the article.

Since in German we usually do not look at the gender of the noun, it is the article that provides information. The best tip is to learn the word always together with its article!

However, some hints can be used to find the right article: e.g., by the meaning or the ending. But beware—there are almost always exceptions !!!

The male (masculine) article "der"

First, it can be distinguished by the gender: "der Mann" (the man), "der Student" (the student), "der Lehrer" (the teacher), "der Junge" (the boy), "der Spezialist" (the specialist).

The meaning can be a hint too – masculine are:

Tageszeiten (time of the day) – der Morgen, der Abend, etc. (the morning, the night)

Jahreszeiten (seasons) – der Sommer, der Winter, etc. (summer, winter)

Wochentage (days of the week) – der Montag, der Mittwoch, der Freitag, etc.

Monate (months) – der April, der Juni, der September, etc.

Wetter (the weather) – der Regen, der Schnee, der Blitz, etc. (the rain, the snow, the lightning)

Himmelsrichtungen (cardinal points) – der Süden, der Westen, der Osten, etc. (the south, the west, the east)

Automarken (car brands) – der VW, der Fiat, der Renault, etc.

Züge (trains) – der ICE, der Regionalexpress, der Bummelzug (the ICE, the regional express, the slow train)

Alkoholische Getränke (alcoholic drinks) – der Wein, der Schnaps, der Gin, etc.

Endings are hints too – masculine are:

-er – der Computer, der Drucker, der Laser, etc. (the computer, the printer, the laser)

-ling – der Schmetterling, der Frühling, der Lehrling, etc. (the butterfly, the spring, the apprentice)

-or – der Professor, der Motor, der Reaktor, etc. (the professor, the engine, the reactor)

-ist – der Journalist, der Pazifist, der Maschinist, etc. (the journalist, the pacifist, the machinist)

-ismus – der Mechanismus, der Journalismus, der Kapitalismus, etc. (the mechanism, journalism, capitalism)

The female (feminine) article "die"

Again, it is possible to differentiate first according to the gender, "die Frau" (the woman), "die Lehrerin" (the teacher – female), "die Professorin" (the professor – female).

There are also other hints – feminine are:

Motorradmarken (motorcycle brands) – die Suzuki, die Harley Davidson, die Triumph

Schiffsnamen (names of ships) – die Queen Elisabeth, die Gorch Fock, die Europa, etc.

Flugzeuge (airplanes) – die Boing, die Concorde, die Robin, etc.

Zahlen (numbers) – die Eins, die Sieben, die Neun, etc.

Blumen (flowers) – die Tulpe, die Rose, die Narzisse, etc.

The endings are hints as well – feminine are:

-e – die Lampe, die Ente, die Tasche, etc. (the lamp, the duck, the bag)

-t – die Fahrt, die Naht, die Tat, etc. (the ride, the seam, the act, etc.)

-ei – die Bäckerei, die Tyrannei, die Wäscherei, etc. (the bakery, the tyranny, the laundry, etc.)

-in (female professions) – die Professorin, die Studentin, die Prinzessin, etc. (the professor, the student, the princess, etc.)

-schaft – die Mannschaft, die Belegschaft, die Freundschaft, etc. (the team, the workforce, the friendship, etc.)

-heit/-keit – die Freiheit, die Einsamkeit, die Möglichkeit, etc. (freedom, loneliness, opportunity, etc.)

-ung – die Zeitung, die Umleitung, die Meinung, etc. (the newspaper, the diversion, the opinion, etc.)

The endings of foreign words are also helpful – feminine are:

-ion – die Aktion, die Diskussion, die Tradition, etc. (the action, the discussion, the tradition)

-age – die Gage, die Passage, die Garage, etc. (the fee, the passage, the garage)

-ur – die Manufaktur, die Agentur, die Partitur, etc. (the manufactory, the agency, the score)

-ik – die Musik, die Physik, die Metrik, etc. (the music, the physics, the metric)

-anz – die Akzeptanz, die Toleranz, die Eleganz, etc. (the acceptance, the tolerance, the elegance)

-tät – die Realität, die Modernität, die Qualität, etc. (the reality, the modernity, the quality)

-ade – die Limonade, die Parade, die Marmelade, etc. (the lemonade, the parade, the jam)

-enz – die Präsenz, die Prominenz, die Tendenz, etc. (the presence, the prominence, the tendency)

The neuter (neutral) article "das"

The meaning gives hints – neutral are:

Farben (colors) – das Blau, das Grün, das Weiß, etc.

Metalle (metals) – das Silber, das Gold, das Eisen, etc.

Chemische Elemente (chemical elements) – das Helium, das Uran, das Neon, etc.

Substantivierte Verben (substantive verb) – das Lesen, das Schlafen, das Schwimmen, etc.(reading, sleeping, swimming)

Substantivierte Adjektive (substantive adjective) – das Schöne, das Gute, das Helle, etc. (the beautiful, the good, the bright)

The endings give hints too – neutral are:

Diminuitive (-chen/-lein) (diminuitive) – das Häuschen, das Mädchen, das Kindlein, etc. (the cottage, the girl, the baby)

-um – das Museum, das Atomium, das Publikum, etc. (the museum, the Atomium, the audience)

-nis – das Ereignis, das Wagnis, das Erlebnis, etc. (the event, the venture, the experience)

-tum – das Ultimatum, das Beamtentum, das Brauchtum, etc. (the ultimatum, the officialdom, the customs)

-ment – das Regiment, das Parlament, das Instrument, etc. (the regiment, the parliament, the instrument)

-o – das Auto, das Motto, das Kino, etc. (the car, the motto, the cinema)

Now that you know some useful hints for the definite articles in German, it is time to learn some more and see how they are used in different situations.

When you stumble upon someone and want to have small talk, you will usually talk about the weather, the time, and some general information about each other. Let's take a look at this conversation between Laura and Mark.

Laura: Hallo, entschuldige bitte. Wann kommt der ICE?

Mark: Hey, ich glaube der kommt um 17 Uhr.

Laura: Ach, okay. Vielen Dank. Ich darf das Konzert in Berlin nicht verpassen.

Mark: Kein Problem. Ich gehe auch auf das Konzert. Du magst also Maroon 5?

Laura: Super. Ja, ich bin ein großer Fan. Ihre Musik ist einfach genial.

Mark: Ja, sie sind klasse. Ich habe sogar ein schwarzes T-Shirt mit ihrem Logo selbst gemacht.

Laura: Wow, sieht echt super aus. Ich würde gerne auch so etwas haben. Du bist wirklich talentiert.

Mark: Danke sehr. Ich studiere Grafikdesign und interessiere mich für Kunst. Ich kann dir auch so ein T-Shirt machen. Was machst du so?

Laura: Cool! Das wäre toll. Ich studiere Medizin. Nicht sehr kreativ, aber ich liebe es den Menschen zu helfen. Es ist meine Leidenschaft.

Mark: Ich finde das sehr interessant und aufregend. Du bist sehr mutig!

Laura: Danke… oh, da kommt der Zug.

Mark: Ja, lass uns schnell einsteigen!

Translation

Laura: Hello, sorry, please. When is the ICE coming?

Mark: Hey, I think it is coming at 5:00 pm.

Laura: Oh, okay. Many Thanks. I cannot miss the concert in Berlin.

Mark: No problem. I am also going to the concert. So you like Maroon 5?

Laura: Great. Yes, I am a big fan. Their music is just awesome.

Mark: Yes, they are great. I even made a black T-shirt with their own logo.

Laura: Wow, it looks really great. I would like to have something like that too. You are really talented.

Mark: Thank you very much. I study graphic design and am interested in art. I can make you a T-shirt as well. What are you doing?

Laura: Cool! That would be great. I study medicine. Not very creative, but I love helping people. It is a passion.

Mark: I think that is very interesting and exciting. You are very brave!

Laura: Thanks... Oh, here comes the train.

Mark: Yes, let's get in fast!

As you can see from the conversation, there are definite articles like "der Zug" (the train), "das Konzert" (the concert). But there are also some other forms like "den Menschen" (the people) and other words like "ein T-Shirt" (a shirt), "eine Leidenschaft" (a passion). This is because we can decline definite articles, and there are also indefinite articles: "ein, eine, ein".

Let's take a look at the declination of definite articles:

N- Nominative

A – Accusative

D – Dative

G – Genitive

Masculine (N) der Mann (A) den Mann (D) dem Mann (G) des Mannes

Der Mann ist 22 Jahre alt. Ich kenne den Mann. Der Stift gehört dem Mann. Das ist der Stift des Mannes.

The man is 28 years old. I know the man. The pen belongs to the man. This is the pen from the man.

Feminine (N) die Frau (A) die Frau (D) der Frau (G) der Frau

Die Frau ist 28 Jahre alt. Ich kenne die Frau. Der Stift gehört der Frau. Das ist der Stift der Frau.

Neutral (N) das Kind (A) das Kind (D) dem Kind (G) des Kindes

Das Kind ist 12 Jahre alt. Ich kenne das Kind. Der Stift gehört dem Kind. Das ist der Stift des Kindes.

Plural (N) die Eltern (A) die Eltern (D) den Eltern (G) der Eltern

Die Eltern sind 30 Jahre alt. Ich kenne die Eltern. Der Stift gehört den Eltern. Das ist der Stift der Eltern.

You got it, right? It is pretty simple, and when you know how the articles change depending on the case, then it is easy to form sentences.

Marcus und Petra sind verheiratet. Ihnen gehört **das Haus**. Sie wohnen in **dem Haus**. In dem Haus wohnen auch **die Kinder**. Das sind die Spielzeuge **der Kinder**. Ihre Katze ist auch in **dem Haus**. **Die Katze** heißt Mia. Das ist der Ball **der Katze**.

Marcus and Petra are married. They own the house. They live in the house. The children live in the house as well. These are the children's toys. Their cat is also in the house. The cat's name is Mia. That is the cat's ball.

There is also another type of articles we need to talk about: indefinite articles.

(der) **ein** – "ein Mann" (masculine)

(das) **ein** – "ein Kind" (neutral)

(die) **eine** – "eine Frau" (feminine)

The use of the indefinite article

The indefinite article is used when speaking about something indeterminate/nonconcrete/indefinite.

Die Katze holt einen Ball – The cat gets a ball. (We do not know which ball; there can be many of them or different ones)

Ich habe eine blaue Jacke – I have a blue jacket. (The person owns a blue jacket, but there may be more)

Du liest ein Buch – You are reading a book. (The person did not say which book or if there is just one)

Declination

Masculine (N) ein Mann (A) einen Mann (D) einem Mann (G) eines Mannes

Ein Mann hat schöne Schuhe. Frage einen Mann. Die Schuhe gehören einem Mann. Es sind die Schuhe eines Mannes.

A man has beautiful shoes. Ask a man. The shoes belong to a man. They are the shoes of a man.

As you can see, we do not know which man. We just know that it is a man. It can be a man on the street, in a movie, in the park or anywhere else. It is not specified.

Feminine (N) eine Frau (A) eine Frau (D) einer Frau (G) einer Frau

Eine Frau hat schöne Schuhe. Frage eine Frau. Die Schuhe gehören einer Frau. Es sind die Schuhe einer Frau.

Neutral (N) ein Kind (A) ein Kind (D) einem Kind (G) eines Kindes

Ein Kind hat schöne Schuhe. Frage ein Kind. Die Schuhe gehören einem Kind. Es sind die Schuhe eines Kindes.

Plural (N) – Eltern (A) – Eltern (D) – Eltern (G) – Eltern

So, as you can see, the endings are similar to the ones from the definite articles.

In some cases, the article is merged with a preposition:

An + das = ans (to) "Ich fahre ans Meer" – I drive to the sea

an + dem = am (on) "Am Montag gehe ich" – I am going on Monday

in + das = ins (into) "Ich springe ins Wasser" – I jump into the water.

in + dem = im (in) "Ich bin im Kino" – I am in the cinema.

zu + der = zur (to) "Ich gehe zur Arbeit" – I am going to work.

zu + dem = zum (to) "Ich gehe zum Kino" – I am going to the cinema.

bei + dem = beim (at) "Ich bin beim Bahnhof" – I am at the station.

There is also a negative article: "**kein**".

It denies nouns without articles and nouns with indefinite articles.

Declination of "kein":

Masculine (N) kein Mann (A) keinen Mann (D) keinem Mann (G) keines Mannes

Feminine (N) keine Frau (A) keine Frau (D) keiner Frau (G) keiner Frau

Neutral (N) kein Kind (A) kein Kind (D) keinem Kind (G) keines Kindes

Plural (N) keine Eltern (A) keine Eltern (D) keinen Eltern (G) keiner Eltern

Examples:

"Das ist Mark."

"Er hat kein Geld."

"Deshalb hat er kein Auto und keine Freundin."

"Das ist Laura. Sie hat kein Interesse an Mark."

Translation

"That is Mark."

"He has no money."

"That is why he does not have a car or a girlfriend."

"That is Laura. She has no interest in Mark."

Don't worry if everything seems complicated. You will practice it with time and learn the articles as you move on. It is important that you learn the article and declination right away.

Let's move on to the next lesson!

Chapter 4 – Education and Work

Quick Overview

- Vocabulary
- Phrases for talking about education and work
- Personal pronouns, possessive pronouns, reflexive pronouns
- Important verbs
- Word order

You now know how to introduce yourself, talk about yourself a bit, tell the time and date, and some other basics of the German language. However, it is important to learn to speak about your education and career, too, because there will come a situation where you will speak with someone about such information. So, let's start!

Vocabulary:

Der Schüler /in – pupil

Die Klasse – grade/class

Das Fach – Subject

Das Lieblingsfach – favorite subject

der Schulleiter – principal

der Student – student

die Universität – university

die Note – grade

das Zeugnis – report

die Ausbildung – education/professional training

die Bildung – education

die Weiterbildung – further training

die Berufsausbildung – vocational training

das Praktikum – internship

die Sekräterin – secretary

die Firma – company

die Bewerbung – application

der Abschluss – graduation

der Angestellte – employee

der Arbeiter – worker

der Arbeitgeber – employer

der Beruf – profession

die Beschäftigung – occupation

der Chef – boss

der Azubi, Lehrling – apprentice, trainee

das Bewerbungsformular – application form

der Lebenslauf – curriculum vitae

der Facharbeiter – skilled worker

die freie Stelle – vacancy

die Lehrstelle, Lehrzeit – apprenticeship

das Vorstellungsgespräch – job interview

die Arbeitslosenunterstützung – unemployment benefit

die Arbeitslosigkeit – unemployment

arbeitslos sein – to be unemployed

die Lohnerhöhung – pay rise

die Gleitzeit – flexitime

die Schicht – shift

der Teilzeitjob – part-time job

die Überstunden – overtime

der Vollzeitjob – full-time job

der/die Apotheker/in – chemist/pharmacist

der/die Arzt/Ärztin – doctor

der/die Astronaut/in – astronaut

der/die Autor/in – author/ess

der/die Bäcker/in – baker

der Bauarbeiter – construction worker

der/die Bauer/Bäuerin – farmer

der Bergarbeiter – miner

der/die Bestatter/in – undertaker

der/die Biologe/Biologin – biologist

der/die Busfahrer/in – bus driver

der/die Chefkoch/Chefköchin – chef

der/die Chirurg/in – surgeon

der/die Dachdecker/in – roofer

der/die Elektriker/in – electrician

der/die Feuerwehrmann/-frau – firefighter

der/die Fernfahrer/in – truck driver

der/die Fitnesstrainer/in – fitness instructor

der/die Fleischer/in – butcher

der/die Florist/in – florist

der/die Forscher/in – research scientist

der/die Friseur/in – hairdresser, hairstylist

der/die Gärtner/in – gardener

der/die Glaser/in – glazier

der/die Grafiker/in – graphic artist/designer

der/die Hausmeister/in – caretaker

der/die Ingenieur/in – engineer

der/die Jäger/in – hunter/huntsman/huntswoman

der/die Journalist/in – journalist

der/die Kellner/in – waiter/waitress

der/die Kindergärtner/in – nursery school teacher

der/die Kinderpfleger/in – childcare assistant

der/die Klempner/in – plumber

der/die Koch/Köchin – cook

der/die Kosmetiker/in – beautician, cosmetician, make-up artist

der/die Kundenberater/in – customer advisor

der/die Krankenschwester/pfleger – nurse

der/die Lehrer/in – teacher

der/die Maler/in – painter

der/die Maurer/in – bricklayer, brickie

der/die Mechaniker/in – mechanic

der/die Modell – (fashion) model

der/die Modedesigner/in – fashion designer

der/die Physiotherapeut/in – physiotherapist

der/die Pilot/in – pilot

der/die Polizist/in – police officer

der/die Reiseleiter/in – tour guide

der/die Sanitäter/in – paramedic

der/die Sänger/in – singer; vocalist

der/die Schäfer/in – shepherd/ess

der/die Schauspieler/in – actor/actress

der/die Schornsteinfeger/in – (chimney) sweep

die Sekretärin – secretary

der/die Sozialarbeiter/in – social worker

der/die Taxifahrer/in – taxi/cab driver

der/die Techniker/in – engineer

der/die Tierarzt / Tierärztin – vet

der/die Tischler/in – carpenter

der/die Trainer/in – coach, trainer

der/die Verkäufer/in – shop assistant

der/die Zahnarzt / Zahnärztin – dentist

der/die Zoologe / Zoologin – zoologist

Now that you are familiar with the important nouns for this lesson let's move on to conversation.

Phrases for talking about education and work:

Bist du ein Schüler? – Are you a pupil?

Ja, ich bin ein Schüler – I am a pupil. (male)

Ich bin eine Schülerin – I am a pupil. (female)

Note: In German, the ending "in" is being added for feminine nouns. Example: (m)Lehrer – (f)Lehrerin; (m)Assistent – (f)Assistentin.

Ich bin in der Grundschule/Hauptschule/Realschule/Gymnasium – I am in elementary school/high school/junior high school/gymnasium.

Ich gehe auf die _____ (Name der Schule/Institution) – I go to the _____(name of the school/institution).

Ich bin in der ersten Klasse – I am in the first grade.

Mein Lieblingsfach ist Deutsch/Biologie/Mathematik – My favorite subject is German/biology/math.

Ich liebe/hasse die Schule – I love/hate school.

Ich finde den Lehrer/die Lehrerin toll – I think the teacher is great.

Der Schulleiter heißt... – The name of the principal is….

Ich habe sehr gute Noten – I have very good grades.

Ich habe schlechte Noten – I have bad grades.

Ich bin Student/Studentin – I am a student.

Ich gehe auf die Universität – I go to the college.

Ich studiere Philosophie/Medizin/Informatik – I study philosophy/medicine/informatics.

Ich möchte mich einschreiben – I want to sign in.

Ich interessiere mich für Kunst – I am interested in art.

Ich bin im dritten Jahr – I am in the third year.

Ich möchte mein Zeugnis bekommen – I want to get my report.

Hast du zurzeit Prüfungen? Wie geht es so? – Do you have any exams at the moment? How is it going?

Ich habe gerade meinen Bachelor abgeschlossen – I have just completed my Bachelor.

Ich mache meinen master in chemistry – I am doing a masters in chemistry.

Hast du studiert? – Did you study?

Nein, das habe ich nicht. Ich mache gerade eine Ausbildung – No, I have not. I am doing an apprenticeship.

Ich bin daran nicht interessiert – I am not interested in that.

Wo bist du zur Universität gegangen? – Where did you go to university?

Was hast du studiert? – What did you study?

Wenn ich meinen Abschluss habe, möchte ich Kunst studieren – When I finish school, I want to study art.

Ich mache eine Ausbildung zum Arzt – I am doing an education/professional training to become a doctor.

Ich mache eine Berufsausbildung. Es dauert noch einige Monate und dann bin ich fertig damit – I am doing vocational training. It lasts a few more months and then I am done with it.

Ich mache eine Ausbildung – I am taking vocational training.

Ich muss ein Praktikum abschließen – I need to complete an internship.

Ich arbeite als Sekräterin – I am working as a secretary.

Die Arbeit des Feuerwehrmanns kann sehr gefährlich sein – The job of a fireman can be very dangerous.

Die Arbeit mit Kindern macht mir Spaß – The work with kids is fun.

Manchmal ist die Arbeit langweilig – Sometimes work can be boring.

Ich arbeite in einer Firma – I work in a company.

Meine Firma ist sehr groß/klein – My company is very big/small.

Ich arbeite in einer Firma mit zehn Leuten – I work in a company with ten people.

Mein Boss ist gut/schlecht – My boss is good/bad.

Ich muss eine Bewerbung abschicken – I need to send my application.

Ich möchte gerne als Architekt arbeiten – I want to work as an architect.

Ich bin sehr fleißig/motiviert/selbstständig – I am very hardworking/motivated/independent.

Ich bin selbstständig, aber kann auch im Team arbeiten – I am independent, but I can work in a team as well.

Ich würde mich gerne für die Stelle____ bewerben – I would like to apply for the position of the _____.

Ich möchte eine Lohnerhöhung – I want a pay rise.

Kann ich hier eine Berufsausbildung machen? – Can I take vocational training here?

Kann ich ein Bewerbungsformular haben? – Can I have an application form?

Hier ist mein Lebenslauf – Here is my CV.

Ich habe um 10 Uhr ein Vorstellungsgespräch – I have a job interview at 10 o'clock.

Ich bin zur Zeit arbeitslos – I am unemployed at the moment.

Ich bin auf der Suche nach einem Job – I am searching for a job.

Gibt es hier Schichten? – Are there shifts here?

Ich suche nach einem Teilzeitjob – I am looking for a part-time job.

Ich suche nach einem Vollzeitjob – I am looking for a full-time job.

Ich möchte kündigen – I want to quit.

Ich möchte etwas anderes finden – I want to find something else.

Haben Sie eine freie Stelle? – Do you have a free spot?

When you want to ask someone about their education/work/career:

Wo gehst du zur Schule? – Where do you go to school?

Wo bist du zur Schule gegangen? – Where did you go to school?

Was studierst du? – What do you study?

Woran bist du interessiert? – What are you interested in?

In welchem Jahr bist du? – What year are you in?

Wann machst du deinen Abschluss? – When will you graduate?

Was ist dein Lieblingsfach? – What is your favorite subject?

Wo arbeitest du? – Where do you work?

Gefällt dir dein Job? – Do you like your job?

Was möchtest du werden? – What do you want to become?

Was möchtest du in der Zukunft machen? – What do you want to do in the future?

Hast du irgendwelche Pläne? – Do you have any plans?

Now that you know some of the basic phrases, we need to go back to the grammar. You may have noticed some words like *mein, meine, dein…* and if you remember the phrase "Wie geht es dir/ Ihnen?" – "How are you?" then you may have also noticed the word "dir".

If you are asking yourself what that means, don't worry—we will explain it right now. These words are pronouns, and there are different types.

First, are **PERSONAL PRONOUNS**.

Personal pronouns replace the nouns in the sentence. This makes the sentence shorter, and repeating of nouns is avoided.

Examples:

Der Hund ist sehr schön. **Er** heißt Tom – **The dog** is really beautiful. **His** name is Tom.

Der Schrank ist sehr modern. Er kostet 300 EUR – The cupboard is very modern. It is 300 Eur.

Personal pronouns are declined in the **dative** and **accusative**.

Dative

Mir, dir, ihm, ihr, ihm

Uns, euch, ihnen

Accusative

Mich, dich, ihn, sie, es

Uns, euch, sie

Examples:

Schön dich kennen zu lernen – It is nice to meet you.

Wir haben uns nie gesehen – We never saw each other.

Wie geht es dir? – How are you?

Mir geht es gut – I am good.

Mein Rücken tut mir weh – My back hurts.

A second type of pronoun are **POSSESSIVE PRONOUNS**.

Possessive pronouns determine ownership. If you want to say that something is yours or belongs to someone else, you will say:

Das ist **meine** Tasche – This is **my** bag.

Das ist dein Buch – This is your book.

Wo sind eure Sachen? – Where is your stuff?

<u>Possessive pronouns:</u>

Ich – mein

Du – dein

Er – sein

Sie – ihr

Es – sein

Wir – unser

Ihr – euer

Sie – ihr

Possessive pronouns are declined and receive the following endings:

Nominative

Maskulin - / ; feminine –e; neutral -/; Plural –e.

Example:

Das ist mein Auto. (This is my car)

Das ist seine Frau. (This is his wife)

Das ist euer Kind. (This is your child)

Genitive

Masculine - es ; feminine –er; neutral -es; Plural –er.

Example:

Die Stühle

Der Preis seines Stuhles ist hoch. (The price of his chair is high.)

Die Schuhe

Der Preis ihrer Schuhe ist hoch. (The price of her shoes is high)

Das Telefon

Der Preis seines Telefons ist hoch. (The price of his telephone is high)

Dative

Masculine - em ; feminine –er; neutral -em; Plural –en.

Example:

Ich gehe zu meinem Freund. (I am going to my boyfriend.)

Ich gehe zu meiner Freundin. (I am going to my girlfriend.)

Ich gehe zu meinem Fahrrad. (I am going to my bicycle.)

Accusative

Masculine - en ; feminine –e; neutral -/; Plural –e.

Example:

Er ruft seinen Vater. (He calls his father)

Seine Bücher wurden gestohlen. (His books were stolen.)

Sein Auto ist kaputt. (His car is broken.)

The third type of pronoun is **REFLEXIVE PRONOUNS** which are: mich, mir, dich, dir, sich, uns, euch, and sich. They are used with reflexive and reciprocal verbs. They always relate to the subject.

Example:

Ich wasche **mir** die Hände – I wash **my** hands.

Wir treffen **uns** – We meet each other.

Reflexive pronouns depend on the subject and must be declined:

Reflexive pronouns can only stand in the accusative and the dative and differ there only in the first and second person singular.

Nominative

Ich, du, er, sie, es

Wir, ihr, sie

Accusative

Mich, dich, sich

Uns, euch, sich

Ich wasche mich – I wash myself.

Dative

Mir, dir, sich

Uns, euch, sich

Ich gehe zu dir – I am going to you.

And here are the important verbs from the lesson and how you should conjugate them:

arbeiten – to work

machen – to do

sich interessieren – to be interested in something/someone

studieren – to study

The verb "arbeiten" is conjugated regularly by adding the endings to the verb stem.

ich arbeite

du arbeitest

er, sie, es arbeitet

wir arbeiten

ihr arbeitet

sie arbeiten

It is the same with **machen and studieren**.

But when it comes to the verb "interessieren", there can be some changes.

Some verbs require the reflexive pronoun "sich" (yourself).

sich beeilen – hurry yourself up

sich interessieren – to interest yourself

sich fühlen – to feel yourself

The reflexive pronoun can mean that the activity is directed to the subject.

sich waschen – to wash yourself

Das Mädchen wäscht sich – The girl washes herself.

sich verletzen – to hurt yourself

Ich habe mich verletzt – I have hurt myself.

The **reflexive verb** must be conjugated.

sich interessieren

ich interessiere mich (für Kunst) – I am interested (in art).

du interessierst dich

er, sie, es interessiert sich

wir interessieren uns

ihr interessiert euch

sie interessieren sich

If the reflexive verb requires an accusative object, the reflexive pronoun changes:

ich wasche mir die Haare – I am washing my hair.

du wäschst dir die Haare.

er, sie, es wäscht sich die Haare.

wir waschen uns die Haare.

ihr wascht euch die Haare.

sie waschen sich die Haare.

In addition to reflexive use, some verbs can also be used to denote a reciprocal relationship that always involves at least two people. Therefore, the verb and the reciprocal pronoun are always in the plural.

Reciprocal verbs occur only with subjects in the plural. Therefore, the plural forms of the reflexive pronoun are used: uns, euch, and sich.

sich kennenlernen → Wir haben uns in der High School kennengelernt – We met in high school.

sich gut verstehen → Wir haben uns sofort gut verstanden – We immediately got on well with each other.

sich begrüßen → Herr Müller und seine Nachbarin begrüßen sich jeden Morgen auf der Straße – Mr. Müller and his neighbor greet each other every morning on the street.

Before we move on, we need to explain some more things when it comes to **WORD ORDER**.

There are some specific situations when it comes to asking questions. We are talking about "Welch-Questions" or "What-Questions".

"Welch- question" is used in choosing a particular person or thing among others.

"Welch-question" is before the noun, not the article.

"Welch-question" is being declined like a definite article.

Nominative

Masculine: welcher Tisch?; welcher Rock? (what table? what skirt?)

Feminine: welche Lampe?; welche Jacke? (what lamp? what jacket?)

Neutral: welches Bett? welches Kleid? (what bed? what dress?)

Plural: welche Stühle? (what chairs?)

Welcher Rock gefällt dir? – (what skirt do you like?)

Genitive

Masculine:welchen Tisches?; welchen Rockes?

Feminine: welcher Lampe?; welcher Jacke?

Neutral:welchen Bettes?; welchen Kleides?

Plural:welcher Stühle?; welcher Schuhe?

Das Licht welcher Lampe stört dich? – The light of what lamp is bothering you?

Dative

Masculine:welchem Tisch?; welchem Rock?

Feminine:welcher Lampe?; welcher Jacke?

Neutral:welchem Bett?; welchem Kleid?

Plural:welchen Stühlen?; welchen Schuhen?

Zu welchen Schuhen passt diese Bluse? – To which shoes does this blouse fit?

Accusative

Masculine:welchen Tisch?; welchen Rock?

Feminine:welche Lampe?; welche Jacke?

Neutral:welches Bett?; welches Kleid?

Plural:welche Stühle?; welche Schuhe?

Welches Kleid soll ich anziehen? – What dress should I wear?

We also need to go over **CAUSAL SENTENCES** with "weil" (because).

The conjunction "weil" or because denotes a cause. After the conjunction follows a subordinate clause (the subject + other clauses + the predicate at the end). If the weil-sentence comes first, then the main clause must begin with the predicate.

Ich gehe heute nicht zur Schule, weil ich sehr krank bin – I am not going to school today because I am very sick.

Weil ich sehr krank bin, bleibe ich heute zu Hause – Because I am very sick, I am staying at home today.

Wir werden uns beeilen weil wir um 7 Uhr dort sein müssen – We will hurry up because we need to be there at 7 o'clock.

Ich bin schlecht gelaunt weil ich kein Geld habe – I am in a bad mood because I do not have money.

Now we will move on to **SENTENCES** with **DASS**.

We will first go over object sentences with dass (that).

The object sets begin with the conjunction "dass". After the conjunction, the subordinate clause (the subject + other clauses + the predicate) follows.

Sie hat gesagt dass sie nicht kommen kann – She said that she can not come.

Wir wissen schon, dass wir zu spät gekommen sind – We already know that we came late.

Bist du sicher dass Patrick im Haus isst? – Are you sure that Patrick is in the house?

Some subordinate clauses represent a phrase. That is why they are called limb sets.

If, as in this case, a subordinate clause stands in the place of an object, this is called an object sentence. The subordinate clause thus has the function of an accusative object of the main clause.

The question for an object sentence is the same as for an object.

Was weißt du? – Ich weiß, dass du sehr gut singen kannst – What do you know? – I know that you can sing very well.

Was hast du erfahren? – Ich habe erfahren, dass es eine Party am Freitag gibt – What did you find out? – I have found out that there is a party on Friday.

Subject sentences with "dass".

If a subordinate clause stands in the place of a subject, one calls this a subject sentence. A subject-sentence indicates information about the subject of a sentence, and we can ask the questions "wer" or "was" (who or what).

Mein größter Wunsch ist, dass ich Arzt werde – Was ist mein größter Wunsch? – Dass ich Arzt werd – My biggest wish is that I become a doctor – What is my biggest wish? – That I become a doctor.

Dass die Sonne nicht scheint, ist sehr schade – Was ist sehr schade? – Dass die Sonne nicht scheint – That the sun is not shining is a great pity – What is a pity? – That the sun is not shining.

We will now go over the **Indirect questions.**

The questions may appear as subordinate clauses in the compound sentences.

In the subordinate clause from the supplementary question (with a question word at the beginning) the predicate is at the end.

Was hast du heute gemacht? – What did you do today?

Ich habe gefragt was du heute gemacht hast – I asked what you did today.

Ich würde gerne wissen, wann dieser Laden aufmacht – I would really like to know when this shop is opening.

The subordinate clause from the decision question begins with the conjunction "ob"; the predicate is at the end of the sentence.

Gehst du morgen mit mir?

Ich habe gefragt, ob du morgen mit mir gehst.

Ist die Nummer richtig?

Ich bin nicht sicher, ob die Nummer richtig ist.

Könnten Sie mir bitte Bescheid geben, ob die Reservierung passt? – Could you please let me know if the reservation is all right?

Conditional sentences with "wenn" (if).

The conjunction "wenn" denotes a condition. After the conjunction follows a subordinate clause (the subject + other clauses + the predicate).

Wenn heute die Sonne scheint, gehen wir schwimmen – If today the sun shines, we will go swimming.

Wir gehen schwimmen, wenn heute die Sonne scheint – We go swimming if the sun shines today.

Wenn ich diesen Test nicht bestehe, werde ich viel lernen müssen – If I do not pass this test, I will have to learn a lot.

Wenn Sie etwas kaufen möchten, können Sie sich gerne umschauen – If you want to buy something, you are welcome to look around.

The (unreal) conditional sentences are often in the subjunctive.

Wenn die Sonne heute schiene, würden wir schwimmen gehen – If the sun would shine today, we would go swimming.

Wir würden schwimmen gehen, wenn die Sonne heute schiene – We would go swimming if the sun would shine today.

Sie müssen noch wissen, dass es im Hotel noch schöner wäre wäre das Bett gemütlicher – You should know that it would be even nicer in the hotel if the bed would be comfortable.

Es wäre schön, wenn du die Hausaufgaben bis Mittwoch fertig haben würdest – It would be nice if you could finish the homework by Wednesday.

Wenn Sie noch ein bisschen warten könnten, dann würden Sie ein Ticket bekommen – If you could wait a bit, then you would get a ticket.

Concession sentences with "obwohl" and "trotzdem" (though and anyway).

The concession sentences answer the question "In spite of which counterarguments?"

The concessive sentence can be introduced with the conjunction "obwohl". After the conjunction, the subordinate clause (the subject + other clauses + the predicate) follows.

Obwohl es sehr kalt ist, gehen wir jetzt spazieren – Although it is very cold, we go for a walk now.

Wir gehen spazieren, obwohl es sehr kalt ist – We go for a walk, although it is very cold.

Muss ich auch gehen, obwohl ich keinen Regenmantel habe? – Do I have to go, even though I do not have a raincoat?

Obwohl es nicht verboten ist, stört es mich sehr, wenn ich lerne – Although it is not forbidden, it bothers me a lot when I am learning.

The concessive sentence can also begin with the conjunction "trotzdem". The conjunction requires inversion (the predicate + the subject + other clauses).

Es ist sehr kalt, trotzdem gehen wir spazieren – It is very cold, but we go for a walk anyway.

Ich habe meine Geschwister auf diese Probleme hingewiesen, trotzdem haben sie leider, gar nichts geändert – I pointed out these problems to my siblings, but unfortunately, they have not changed anything.

Consecutive sentences with "deshalb" (therefore).

The conjunction "deshalb" denotes a sequence. The conjunction requires inversion (the predicate + the subject + other clauses).

Ich fühle mich schlecht, deshalb bleibe ich heute zu Hause – I feel bad, that is why I stay at home today.

Sie hatten nicht so viele Probleme, deshalb waren sie sicher weniger gestresst – They did not have that many problems, so they were less stressed out.

Final sentences with "um...zu" and "damit" (in order to, so).

Final sentences answer the question "What for?" and "For what purpose?"

If in both clauses the subjects are equal, the final clause is connected to the main clause by the conjunction "um", after which all other clauses stand, and at the end of the clause the infinitive appears with "zu".

ich = ich

Ich lerne die Sprache. Ich will im Ausland studieren – I learn the language. I want to study abroad.

Ich lerne die Sprache, um im Ausland zu studieren – I learn the language to study abroad.

Drei Freunde fahren in die Berge, um Ski zu fahren – Three friends go to the mountains to go skiing.

In an "in order...to-sentence", the modal verb "wollen" is not there.

Maya sieht sich oft Filme an. Sie will mit ihrem Freund darüber reden – Maya often watches movies. She wants to talk to her friend about it.

Maya sieht sich oft Filme an, um mit ihrem Freund darüber zu reden – Maya often watches movies in order to talk to her friend about it.

If the subjects are different in both clauses, the final clause is joined to the main clause by the conjunction "damit". After the conjunction, the subordinate clause follows (the subject + other clauses + at the end follows the predicate).

ich ≠ mein Lehrer

Ich lerne die Sprache. Mein Lehrer soll zufrieden sein – I learn the language. My teacher should be satisfied.

Ich lerne die Sprache, damit mein Lehrer zufrieden ist – I am learning the language so that my teacher is satisfied.

That is the end of this lesson. If you are ready, let's move on!

Chapter 5 – Family and Friends

Quick overview

- Vocabulary
- Phrases to talk about family and friends
- Important verbs
- Separable and inseparable verbs
- Past tense: preterite and perfect

Family and friends play a crucial role in everyone's life. One of the main topics when doing small talk is definitely the family, and therefore it is important to know how to express yourself and say if you have siblings and how your parents are. It is also important for you to know how to describe your best friend or your friendship group. In this lesson, you will learn the most important phrases and vocabulary when it comes to this topic.

First, you need to know the names of family members in German.

Vocabulary

die Familienmitglieder – family members

die Mutter – mother

der Vater – father

die Eltern – parents

die Ehefrau – wife

der Mann – man

der Sohn – son

die Tochter – daughter

die Kinder – children

der Bruder – brother

die Schwester – sister

die Geschwister – siblings

der Cousin/ die Cousine – cousin

die Verwandtschaft – relatives

die Tante – aunt

der Onkel – uncle

der Neffe – nephew

die Nichte – niece

die Großeltern – grandparents

die Oma – grandmother

der Großvater – grandfather

der Enkel – grandson

die Enkelin – granddaughter

die Enkelkinder – grandchildren

die Schwiegereltern (Schwiegermutter, Schwager etc.) – in-laws

der Ehepartner – spouse

die Stiefmutter/der Stiefvater – stepmother/stepfather

der Stiefsohn/die Stieftochter – stepson /stepdaughter

---

die Stiefschwester/der Stiefbruder – stepsister/stepbrother

die Halbschwester – half-sister

der Halbbruder – half-brother

die Familie – family

die Gegend – area

der Freund – the friend (can also be the boyfriend)

die Freundin – the female friend (can also be the girlfriend)

die Freunde – the friends

der Freundeskreis – the friend group

die beste Freundin/der beste Freund – the best friend

Other important words for this lesson:

Since we often describe ourselves and our family members or friends, we need to know the body parts.

die Körperteile – body parts

das Gesicht – face

das Auge – eye

die Augen – eyes

das Haar – hair

die Haare – hair

die Augenbrauen – eyebrows

der Mund – mouth

die Lippen – lips

die Nase – nose

das Nasenloch – nostril

das Kinn – chin

das Ohr – ear

die Ohren – ears

die Stirn – forehead

die Wange – cheek

die Wimpern – eyelashes

der Zahn – tooth

die Zähne – teeth

die Zunge – tongue

der Arm – arm

die Ärme – arms

der Bauch – stomach

das Bein – leg

die Beine – legs

die Brust – breast

der Ellenbogen – elbow

der Hals – neck

der Kopf – head

das Knie – knee

der Rücken – back

die Schulter – shoulder

die Hand – hand

das Handgelenk – wrist

die Faust – fist

der Finger – finger

der Daumen – thumb

der Fuß – foot

der Zeh – toe

die Wade – calf

der Po – bottom

Now let's look at some things you could say about your family in a simple conversation.

When you want to describe the size of your family and the number of family members:

Ich komme aus einer kleinen/großen Familie – I come from a small/big family.

Es gibt (Anzahl) Personen in meiner Familie – There are (number) people in my family.

Mein Bruder/meine Schwester (Name) lebt in Berlin. Er/Sie ist (Beruf) – My brother/sister (name) lives in Berlin. He/She is an (occupation).

When you want to describe whom you look like and how you or your family members look:

Ich sehe aus wie mein Vater. Wir haben beide braune Augen und schwarzes Haar – I look like my dad. We both have brown eyes and black hair.

Ich bin sehr anders als meine Mutter. Sie ist gesprächig und ungeduldig. Aber ich bin sehr schüchtern und geduldig – I am very different from my mom. She is talkative and not patient at all. But I am very shy and patient.

Meine Schwester bleibt gerne zu Hause und hört Musik, aber ich bevorzuge Sport im Freien – My sister likes to stay home and listen to music, but I prefer outdoor sports.

Mein Bruder spielt gerne Sport, aber ich lese und schaue lieber Filme – My brother enjoys playing sports, but I prefer reading and watching movies.

Wir essen am Wochenende immer zusammen Mittag. Manchmal machen wir einen Ausflug – We always have lunch together at the weekend. Sometimes we go on a trip.

Wir sehen uns nicht oft, aber ich rufe meine Eltern/Geschwister einmal pro Woche/Tag an – We do not see each other often, but I call my parents/siblings once a week/day.

Ich wohne in der Nähe meines Bruders/Cousine, und wir gehen jede Woche essen – I live near my brother/cousin, and we go out to eat every week.

Mein Bruder lebt weit weg, aber ich besuche ihn jeden Winter – My brother lives far away, but I visit him every winter.

There is really no limit to what you can talk about. Talk about their personality, their looks or the things they like to do.

Meine Oma ist sehr klein. Sie hat graue Haare und blaue Augen. Ihre Beine tun ihr manchmal weh – My grandma is very short. She has gray hair and blue eyes. Her legs hurt sometimes.

Meine Tante besucht uns oft. Sie ist sehr aktiv und sportlich. Sie hat lange Beine und schöne, dünne Arme. Ihr Gesicht ist sehr schön, und sie hat schöne, weiße Zähne – My aunt visits us often. She is very active and athletic. She has long legs and nice, thin arms. Her face is very beautiful, and she has beautiful, white teeth

You can also describe your friends in the same way and talk about them.

Ich habe eine beste Freundin. Sie heißt Maria. Sie ist sehr hübsch. Sie hat lange, dunkle Haare und braune Augen. Ihre Lippen sind sehr voll, und ihre Nase klein. Sie arbeitet zurzeit als Modell. Ich bewundere sie deswegen – I have a best friend. She is called Maria. She is very pretty. She has long, dark hair and brown eyes. Her lips are very full, and her nose is small. She is currently working as a model. I admire her for that.

Ich gehe oft mit meinem Freund Fußball spielen. Er ist sehr cool. Wir trainieren zusammen, und ich finde, er ist sehr talentiert. Er ist auch ziemlich schnell – I often go to play football with my friend. He is very cool. We train together, and I think he is very talented. He is also pretty fast.

You can also ask someone about their family or friends.

Geht es deinen Eltern gut? – Are your parents doing well?

Lebst du noch bei deinen Eltern? – Do you still live with your parents?

Lebst du in der Nähe von deinen Familienmitgliedern? – Do you live near any family members?

Wo wohnt deine Familie? – Where does your family live?

Siehst du deine Familie häufig? – Do you see your family frequently?

Wie ist deine Mutter/dein Vater/deine Schwester/dein Bruder, usw.? – How is your mother/father/sister/brother, etc., like?

Hast du einen besten Freund/Freunde? – Do you have a best friend/friends?

Was machst du so mit deinen Freunden? – What do you do with your friends?

Möchtest du etwas mit mir unternehmen? – Do you want to do something?

You can respond easily:

Meinen Eltern geht es gut – My parents are doing well.

Mein Vater wird alt, aber sonst ist er gesund – My father is getting old, but otherwise, healthy.

Meine Mutter hat sich über Herzschmerzen beschwert. Ich hoffe, es ist nichts Ernstes – My mother has been complaining about heart pain. I hope it is not anything serious.

Ja. Ich lebe mit meinen Eltern zusammen – Yeah. I live with my parents.

Nur noch ein Jahr, bis ich wieder auf die Beine komme – Just for another year until I get back on my feet.

Ich bin vor einigen Jahren ausgezogen. Ich habe jetzt eine eigene Wohnung – No. I moved out several years ago. I have my own apartment now.

Meine Familie lebt in München – My family is in Munich.

Meine Familie lebt in der Gegend, daher sehe ich sie normalerweise einmal im Monat – My family lives in the area, so I usually see them once a month.

Mein Vater ist sehr groß, und auf den ersten Blick scheint er sehr streng zu sein – My father is very tall, and he seems strict at first.

Meine Schwester ist sehr schön und klug – My sister is very beautiful and smart.

Mein Bruder ist schlecht in der Schule, aber er ist sehr talentiert, wenn es um Musik geht – My brother is bad at school, but he is very talented when it comes to music.

Besides family, there are always friends who are a great conversation topic. Take a look at these phrases:

Wie lange seid ihr schon Freunde? – How long have you been friends?

Wie lange kennt ihr euch? – Since when do you know each other? Seid ihr zusammen aufgewachsen? – Did you grow up together?

Seid ihr zusammen zur Schule gegangen? – Did you go to school together?

Wie habt ihr euch kennengelernt? – So how did you meet?

Respond like this:

Wir sind Freunde seit der High School – We have been friends since high school.

Ich denke, es ist schon 15 Jahre her – I think it has been like 15 years.

Wir sind zusammen aufgewachsen. Unsere Eltern lebten ziemlich nahe, also waren wir praktisch Nachbarn – We grew up together. Our parents lived pretty close, so we were basically neighbors.

Wir sind seit der 6. Klasse in dieselbe Schule gegangen – We have been in the same school since grade 6.

Wir haben uns in der Grundschule kennengelernt und sind auf die gleiche Schule gegangen – We met in elementary school and started going to the same high school.

Wir fingen an, an dieselbe Universität zu gehen – We started going to the same university.

Wir haben uns auf einer Party kennengelernt. Wir sind seitdem enge Freunde – We met at a party. We have been close friends since.

Wir haben uns in der High School im Matheunterricht kennengelernt – We met in high school in our math class.

Important verbs

geben – to give

leben – to live

sehen – to see

bleiben – to stay

spielen – to play

gehen – to go

ausziehen – to move away

einziehen – to move in

aufwachsen – to grow up

kennenlernen – to meet

You need to know that there can be some exceptions and differences when it comes to verbs and how they are conjugated. The verb-stem of some verbs is changing when we conjugate them. For example the verb: geben – to give.

geb-en (e → i)

ich gebe

du gibst

er, sie, es gibt

wir geben

ihr gebt

sie geben

Du gibst ihm den Ball – You give him the ball.

It is the same with the verb nehmen – to take.

nehm-en

ich nehme

du nimmst

er, sie, es nimmt

wir nehmen

ihr nehmt

sie nehmen

Sie nimmt das Buch – She takes the book.

The verbs "leben, bleiben, spielen, gehen" are being conjugated regularly like the verbs "kommen, heißen, wohnen" and most of the other verbs.

But the verb "sehen" is facing some changes:

seh-en (e → ie)

ich sehe

du siehst

er, sie, es sieht

wir sehen

ihr seht

sie sehen

Du siehst fern – You watch TV.

Something very important and common in the German language is **separable verbs**.

There are separable and inseparable verbs.

Separable verbs consist of the prefix and the verb.

Examples

ausziehen

aus + ziehen

einkaufen – to shop

ein + kaufen

verstehen – to understand

ver + stehen

Ich gehe gleich einkaufen – I will go shop.

Ich kaufe nicht so gern ein – I do not like to shop.

Er sieht elegant aus – He looks elegant.

Ich muss ausziehen – I need to move out.

Ich ziehe morgen aus – I am moving out tomorrow.

The prefix modifies the meaning of the verb. ("aufwachsen" has something to do with "wachsen". "Einkaufen" has something to do with "kaufen".)

In the present and past tense, the prefix stands at the end of the sentence.

In the past participle "-ge" stands between the prefix and the verb. However, we will cover the past tenses later.

Here is just an example:

kaufen → ein-**ge**-kauft

There is also the case where we have separable verbs that consist of two verbs: "kennen" and "lernen" = kennenlernen.

Kennenlernen means to meet someone or to get to know someone, but the word consists of two verbs that have two meanings.

"Kennen" means to know and "lernen" means to learn.

Prefixes for separable verbs:

ab-

abfahren – to drive away

an-

ankommen , anprobieren – to arrive, to try on

auf-

aufstehen – to get up

aus-

aussehen – to look like

bei-

beibringen – to teach

ein-

einpacken – to pack

los-

losgehen – to go

mit-

mitkommen – to come along

nach-

nachmachen – to mimic

vor-

vorstellen – to introduce

zu-

zumachen – to close

There are also **inseparable verbs.**

The prefix here is unstressed.

Ich kann das nicht <u>verstehen</u> – I cannot understand this.

The prefix changes the meaning of the verb. (Verstehen has nothing to do with "stehen" – to stand.)

In the present tense and the preterite, the prefix stands together with the verb.

Ich verstehe das nicht – I do not understand this.

bekommen – to get

Ich habe einen neuen Laptop bekommen – I have got a new laptop.

Prefixes for inseparable verbs:

be-

bekommen – to get

ge-

gefallen – to like

emp-

empfehlen – to recommend

ent-

entschuldigen – to apologize

er-

erzählen – to tell

miss-

missbrauchen – to abuse

ver-

verstehen – to understand

zer-

zerstören – to destroy

There are also some other cases, and we will go over them in this section so that you do not get confused in the following chapters.

If the verb stem is ending with: -eln → sammeln (to collect) the "e" is gone in the first person singular (ich) and the first person plural (wir), and in the third person plural (sie) the verb stem gets the ending -n.

sammeln

ich sammle

du sammelst

er, sie, es sammelt

wir sammeln

ihr sammelt

sie sammeln

In some verbs when conjugating them, the vowel changes in the verb stem. The vowel change occurs only in the second person singular (du) and the third person singular (er, sie , es).

a → ä in "schlafen" – to sleep

schlaf-en

ich schlafe

du schläfst

er, sie, es schläft

wir schlafen

ihr schlaft

sie schlafen

Another example:

laufen – to walk/walk fast

lauf-en

ich laufe

du läufst

er, sie, es läuft

wir laufen

ihr lauft

sie laufen

and another one:

tragen – to carry

trag-en

ich trage

du trägst

er, sie, es trägt

wir tragen

ihr tragt

sie tragen

Before we move on to bigger stuff, we also need to cover the past tenses. It is important for you to know the basics. So let's get that done now!

Past Tense

The preterite is past tense and is mostly used in narratives and written texts.

The first and third person in the past tense is always the same.

Regular verbs:

ich –te

du –test

er, sie, es –te

wir -ten

ihr -tet

sie -ten

kaufen – to buy

ich kaufte

du kauftest

er, sie, es kaufte

wir kauften

ihr kauftet

sie kauften

Ich kaufte mir ein Buch – I bought myself a book.

Regular verbs with the verb stem ending:

-t-

arbeiten

-d-

ba**d**en – to bath

-tm-

a**tm**en – to breathe

-chn-

zei**chn**en – to draw

-ffn-

ö**ffn**en – to open

ich -ete

du -etest

er, sie, es -ete

wir -eten

ihr -etet

sie –eten

Ich arbeitete in einer großen Firma – I have worked in a big company.

Du öffnetest die Tür – You opened the door.

Ihr zeichnetet das Haus – You drew the house.

warten – to wait

ich wartete

du wartetest

er, sie, es wartete

wir warteten

ihr wartetet

sie warteten

Sie warteten auf den Zug –They waited for the train.

Irregular verbs

Ich —

Du -st

Er, sie, es —

Wir -en

Ihr -t

Sie -en

Gehen – to go, to walk

ich ging

du gingst

er, sie, es ging

wir gingen

ihr gingt

sie gingen

Sie ging mit John zur Grundschule – She went with John to primary school.

lassen – to let (go)

ich ließ

du ließt

er, sie, es ließ

wir ließen

ihr ließt

sie ließen

Wir ließen ihn laufen – We let him run.

Another past tense is the **PERFECT.**

The perfect (completed presence) we use for completed actions in which the result of the sequence is in the foreground. In the spoken language we often use the perfect instead of the preterite.

In our simple explanation, you will learn the rules for using and creating the perfect.

Example:

Patrik ist gestern mit Anna ins Kino gegangen. Er hat seine Jacke dort vergessen.

Perfect is formed by the conjugated form of the auxiliary verb ("haben" or "sein") and the past participle at the end of the sentence.

Perfect = **haben / sein** + … + **participle perfect**

Participle perfect can also be called participle II. It comes as part of certain verb forms, but - like the participle 1 - can also be used as an adjective, adverb or noun.

The most common use of participle 2 as part of a verb form is the perfect one we use most of the time in everyday life when we tell something that has been experienced. Added to this is the corresponding form of the auxiliary verb "haben" or "sein".

The participle II, also called "middle word", is used for the formation of the perfect.

Gestern **haben** wir einen Test **geschrieben**. - Yesterday we wrote a test.

Der Bus **ist abgefahren**. - The bus drove away.

Ich **habe** mit ihr den ganzen Tag **telefoniert**. – I have talked with her on a phone the whole day.

And now we will take a look at the formation of the verbs.

Regular verbs

We add to the verb stem: prefix "ge" and ending "-t".

machen → ge–mach–t – to do → done

Ich habe die Hausaufgaben gemacht – I did the homework.

kaufen → ge–kauf–t – to buy → bought

Du hast ein Buch gekauft – You have bought a book.

zeigen → ge-zeig-t – to show → shown

Er hat ihr die Tür gezeigt – He has shown her the door.

Ich habe eine Ausbildung gemacht – I have done an apprenticeship.

For verbs whose verb stem ends with "-t-", "-d-", "-tm-", "-chn-", "-ffn-" – Addition to the verb stem: prefix "ge" and suffix "- et ".

warten → ge–wart–et – to wait → have waited

Ich habe den ganzen Tag gewartet – I have waited the whole day.

baden → ge–bad–et – to bath

Er hat gebadet – He took a bath.

atmen → ge–atm–et – to breathe → have breathed

Sie hat schwer geatmet – She breathed heavily.

zeichnen → ge–zeichn–et – to draw → drew

Wir haben das Bild gezeichnet – We drew the photo.

öffnen → ge–öffn-et – to open → have opened

Sie hat mir die Tür geöffnet – She has opened the door for me.

Irregular verbs

There are also irregular verbs like in the English language. The Perfect Participle of the irregular verbs has to be memorized. It usually ends in "-en".

treffen → getroffen – to meet → have met

Wen hast getroffen? – Who did you meet?

denken → gedacht – to think → have thought

Ich habe an dich gedacht – I have thought about you.

Separable verbs

For regular and irregular separable verbs, the prefix "ge" is between the verb prefix and the verb stem.

einkaufen → ein–ge–kauf–t – to shop → have shopped

Ich habe heute eingekauft – I have shopped today.

ausfüllen → aus–ge–füll-t – to fill out → have filled out

Hast du das Formular ausgefüllt? – Did you fill out the form?

aufstehen → auf–ge–stand–en – to stand up → have stood up

Ich bin um 9 Uhr aufgestanden – I stood up at 9 o'clock.

Past participle perfect without "ge"

For regular and irregular inseparable verbs (with: "be", "ge", "emp-", "ent", "er", "miss", "ver", "zer") there is no prefix "ge".

bestehen → bestand–en – to pass → have passed

Ich habe die Prüfung bestanden – I have passed the exam.

gefallen → gefall–en – to like → have liked

Dir hat das Spiel gefallen – You have liked the game.

empfinden → empfund–en – to feel → have felt

Wir haben Glück empfunden – We have felt luck.

entschuldigen → entschuldig–t – to apologize → have apologized

Ich habe mich bei dir entschuldigt – I have apologized to you.

erzählen → erzähl–t – to tell → have told

Er hat mir eine Geschichte erzählt – He has told me a story.

missbrauchen → missbrauch–t – to abuse → have abused

Sie hat sein Vertrauen missbraucht – She has abused his trust.

verstehen → verstand–en – to understand → have understood

Ich habe es verstanden – I have understood it.

As you can see, it is not that hard, and you will get better when it comes to past tense as you go. Try to remember the verbs and their forms in the perfect as you go through the lessons. You will be able to memorize and practice it.

Chapter 6 – Leisure and Art

Quick Overview

- Vocabulary

- Phrases to talk about leisure, hobbies, and art

- Important verbs: Modal verbs

- Adjectives

- Strong and weak declination

- Positive, Comparative, Superlative

Leisure and art are great conversation topics, and you will certainly be in a situation where you will need to express what you like to do in your free time and what you prefer. It is more about expressing your likes, dislikes, and hobbies, so make sure to follow this lesson and learn some important phrases and vocabulary.

Vocabulary

die Freizeit – leisure, free time

die Freizeitaktivität – recreational activity

das Hobby – hobby

der Spaß – fun

die Computerspiele – computer games

der Fernseher – television

die Zeichnung – drawing

die Musik – music

der Spaziergang – walk

das Kino – cinema

der Fußball – football

der Basketball – basketball

der Tennis – tennis

der Sport – sport

das Café – café

das Buch – book

der Film – film, movie

das Shoppen/Einkaufen – shopping

das Instrument – instrument

das Klavier – piano

die Flöte – flute

die Gitarre – guitar

die Geige – violin

das Haustier – pet

das Wochenende – weekend

die Beschäftigung – activity

die Gartenarbeit – gardening

das Joggen – jogging

das Radfahren – biking, cycling

das Reiten – riding

das Skifahren – skiing

das Schwimmen – swimming

das Segeln – sailing

das Tauchen – diving

das Kegeln – bowling

das Grillen – grilling

der Besuch – visit

der Ausflug – trip

das Museum – museum

das Konzert – concert

die Diskothek – disco

der Zoo – zoo

die Erholung – recreation

das Schach – chess

der Bummel – stroll

das Theater – theater

Now that you know the most important nouns let's take a look at some phrases you could use when talking to someone about your hobbies.

We could simply imagine that you are talking with someone about what you like to do and what you do in your free time. It is great for conversations and bonding with someone. You may find some things you have in common with the other person. So let's start with asking the person what she or he is up to.

Hast du für heute etwas geplant? – Have you planned anything for today?

Ja, ich gehe heute Abend ins Kino – Yes, I am going to the cinema tonight.

Ich schaue mir den neuen Film von Kevin Hart an. Ich liebe seine Komödien – I am watching the new movie with Kevin Hart. I love his comedies.

Ich bin kein Fan von Komödien. Ich mag lieber Actionfilme – I am not a fan of comedies. I like action movies more.

Ins Kino gehe ich nicht sehr oft. Ich bin eher sportlich und mag es in meiner Freizeit ins Fitnessstudio zu gehen. Es entspant mich, und dabei achte ich auch auf meine Gesundheit – I do not go to the cinema very often. I am more athletic and like to go to the gym in my free time. It relaxes me, and I also pay attention to my health.

Was machst du in deiner Freizeit? – What do you do in your free time?

Wie verbringst du das Wochenende? – How do you spend your weekend?

Wann hast du frei? – When are you free?

Ich bin meistens am Wochende frei und verbringe es mit meiner Familie/Freunden. Ich gehe fischen oder in die Berge – I am usually free on weekends and spend it with my family/friends. I go fishing or in the mountains.

Meine Freizeit nutze ich, um mich zu entspannen. Ich gehe manchmal zu einem Yoga-Kurs, meditiere oder lese ein Buch. Ich gehe auch manchmal nach draußen und spaziere einfach ein bisschen – I use my free time to relax. I sometimes go to a yoga class, meditate or read a book. I also go outside sometimes and just walk a bit.

In meiner Freizeit male oder zeichne ich gerne. Ich höre Musik und singe und tanze dazu. Es macht mir viel Spaß – In my spare time I like to paint or draw. I listen to music and sing and dance. I really enjoy it.

Was ist dein Lieblingshobby? – What is your favorite hobby?

Wofür interessierst du dich? – What are you interested in?

Was sind deine Hobbies? – What are your hobbies?

Hast du ein Hobby? – Do you have a hobby?

Ja, ich habe sehr viele Hobbies. Einige davon sind das Schwimmen und Volleyball spielen. Ich mag es aber auch, mit meinen Freunden Brettspiele zu spielen – Yes, I have a lot of hobbies. Some of them are swimming and playing volleyball. I also like to play board games with my friends.

Ich mag es, Musik zu hören. Es entspannt mich, und ich interessiere mich für viele Rock-Bands. Ich mag die Rolling Stones und Aerosmith. Manchmal höre ich mir ihre Musik den ganzen Tag lang an – I like to listen to music. It relaxes me, and I am interested in many rock bands. I like the Rolling Stones and Aerosmith. Sometimes I listen to their music all day long.

Am Wochenende gehe ich gerne mit meinen Freunden zum See. Ich mag die Natur. Wir campen dort und machen ein Lagerfeuer. Dort essen wir etwas und erzählen uns am Abend interessante Geschichten. Wir lachen viel und entspannen uns so – On the weekend I like to go to the lake with my friends. I like nature. We hang out there and make a campfire. There we eat something and tell interesting stories in the evening. We laugh a lot and relax.

Ich interessiere mich für Vögel. Ich mag es, sie zu beobachten und zu analysieren. Sie sind sehr schön und mich faszinieren am meisten Papageie – I am interested in birds. I like watching and analyzing them. They are very beautiful and I am fascinated by parrots.

Fußballspielen macht mir Spaß. Damit bleibe ich in Form und nutze meine Energie – I enjoy playing football. That keeps me in shape and I use my energy.

Eines meiner Hobbys ist das Kochen. Ich liebe es zu essen, doch das Kochen macht mir noch mehr Spaß. Einmal die Woche wähle ich ein

Rezept aus und experimentiere in der Küche. Meine Familie liebt es, wenn ich koche – One of my hobbies is cooking. I love to eat, but cooking is even more fun. Once a week I choose a recipe and experiment in the kitchen. My family loves it when I cook.

Here are some other options for you to talk about what you want, like or do not like.

Ich hatte eine anstrengende Woche und ich möchte mich heute erholen – I had a hard week and I want to relax today.

Ich werde heute einen Film gucken – I will watch a movie today.

Ich habe heute/am Wochenende frei – I am free today/on the weekend.

Ich will heute Abend ins Kino gehen und in ein Restaurant essen gehen – I want to go to the cinema tonight and go to eat in a restaurant.

Ich habe viele Interessen – I have many interests.

Ich interessiere mich für Musik/Sport – I am interested in music/sports.

Ich spiele Gittare und gehe oft ins Kino – I play the guitar and I often go to the cinema.

Ich beschäftige mich auch mit… – I also occupy myself with…

Das macht Spaß – That is fun.

Das finde ich interessant – I find this interesting.

Ich fahre auch Rad – I ride the bike too.

Das ist gesund und kostet nichts – It is healthy and it does not cost anything.

Ich gehe nie einkaufen – I never go shopping.

Das finde ich langweilig – I find that boring.

Meine Hobbies sind Segeln und Skifahren – My hobbies are sailing and skiing.

Ich fahre Ski zweimal im Monat/von Zeit zu Zeit/selten – I am skiing two times a month/occasionally/rarely.

Wie hast du gelernt Klavier zu spielen? – How did you learn to play the piano?

Ich habe Klavier gelernt, indem ich als kleines Kind jeden Tag geübt habe – I have learned to play the piano by practicing every day as a child.Mein Lieblingshobby ist Handballspielen. - My favourite hobby is playing handball.

Ich gehe gerne ins Kino. - I like to go to the cinema.

Ich spiele einmal die Woche Basketball. - I play basketball once a week.

Wofür interessierst du dich? – What are you interested in?

Wie oft spielst du Fußball? – How often do you play football?

In meiner Freizeit tanze ich – In my free time I dance.

Ich surfe jeden Tag im Internet – I surf the Internet every day.

Abends sehen wir fern – We watch the TV at night.

Meine Eltern gehen gerne essen – My parents like to go out to eat.

Meine Familie mag es, Campen zu gehen – My family likes to go camping.

Ich habe viele Hobbys – I have many hobbies.

Laura hört gerne Musik – Laura likes to listen to music.

Mark sieht gerne fern – Mark likes to watch the TV.

Ich spiele Basketball am Mittag – I play basketball at noon.

Jeden Morgen vor der Schule lese ich Bücher – Every morning before school I read books.

In meiner Freizeit male ich gerne – I like to paint in my free time.

Ich jogge gerne – I like to jog.

Ich treibe sehr gerne Sport in meiner Freizeit – I like to do sports in my free time.

Ich treibe zweimal pro Woche Sport – I do sports two times a week.

Jeden Sonntag gehe ich schwimmen – I go swimming every Sunday.

Jedes Wochenende gehe ich mit meinem Vater angeln – Each weekend I go fishing with my father.

Ich fotografiere Tiere sehr gerne – I like to take photos of animals.

Ich mag schönes Wetter und die Sonne – I like nice weather and the sun.

Ich faulenze gerne – I like to be lazy.

Meine Schwester und ich unternehmen gerne etwas zusammen – My sister and I like to do something together.

Ich kann sehr gut singen – I can sing very well.

Laura kann gut schreiben – Laura writes well.

Mein kleiner Bruder ist sehr talentiert. Er kann sehr gut Flöte spielen. Manchmal höre ich ihm zu – My little brother is very talented. He can play the flute very well. Sometimes I listen to him.

Mit meinen Freunden gehe ich oft zum Paintball. Es macht sehr viel Spaß – I often go to paintball with my friends. It is a lot of fun.

There will probably be some situations where you will go out and meet new people. Here are some expressions for dates, going out, giving compliments, flirting, and so on. If you want to know how to ask someone for an appointment or to learn some phrases that you can use to impress a woman or man, you will find everything you need here.

If you are in a club and see someone you like, you can simply say:

Hallo, können wir uns kennenlernen? – Hello, can we meet?

Hey, ich beobachte dich schon seit einiger Zeit. Ich finde du siehst toll aus. Ich heiße Patrick. Kann ich deinen Namen wissen? – Hey, I have been watching you for some time. I think you look great. My name is Patrick. Can I know your name?

Hallo, vielen Dank. Ja, gerne. Mein Name ist Sofie – Hello, thank you. Yes, gladly. My name is Sofie.

Schön dich kennenzulernen, Sofie. Kann ich dir einen ausgeben? – Nice to meet you, Sofie. Can I buy you a drink?

Möchtest du etwas trinken? – Would you like a drink?

Soll ich dir etwas zu trinken holen? Sie haben tolle Cocktails hier – Can I get you a drink? They have great cocktails here.

Mit wem bist du hier? – Who are you with?

Ich bin hier mit meinen Freunden – I am here with my friends.

Ich bin alleine unterwegs – I am on my own.

Ich bin mit meiner Freundin hier. Sie ist gerade auf der Toilette – I am here with my friend. She is in the toilet right now.

Ich verstehe. Wenn du willst, kannst du dich zu mir und meinen Freunden setzen? – I see. If you want, can you sit down with me and my friends?

Du kannst gerne zu unserem Tisch kommen, wenn du willst? – You are welcome to come to our table if you want?

Nein, danke. Ich muss hier bleiben – No, thank you. I have to stay here.

Macht es dir was aus, wenn ich bei dir bleibe? – Do you mind if I stay here with you?

Können meine Freunde und ich uns zu euch setzen? – Can my friends and I sit with you?

Kann ich mich setzen? – Can I sit?

Ja, gerne. Du kannst dich hierhin setzen – Yes, gladly. You can sit here.

Kommst du immer hierher? Bist du öfter hier? – Do you always go out here? Do you come here often?

Bist du zum ersten Mal hier? – Is this your first time here?

Warst du schon mal hier? – Have you been here before?

Ja, ich komme ständig hierhin zum Ausgehen. Ich mag die Leute hier – Yes, I always go out here. I like the people here.

Ich bin hier zum ersten Mal. Es ist cool – I am here for the first time. It is cool.

Würdest du gerne tanzen? – Would you like to dance?

Würdest du es ablehnen, wenn ich dich um einen Tanz bitte? – Would you reject me if I asked you for a dance?

Ich würde gerne tanzen. Lass uns loslegen – I would love to dance. Let's go.

Nein, danke. Ich tanze nicht gerne. Ich bin schlecht darin – No, thanks. I do not like to dance. I am bad at it.

Ich mag Tanzen nicht – I do not like dancing.

Möchstest du morgen mit mir was trinken gehen? Ich kenne eine coole Bar in der Stadt – Would you like to have a drink with me tomorrow? I know a cool bar in town.

Ich habe mich gefragt, ob du vielleicht auf einen Drink mitkommst? – I was wondering if you would like to go out for a drink sometime?

Ich würde sehr gerne mal mit dir ausgehen. Was hältst du davon? Hast duZeit? – I would very much like to go out with you. So what do you think about that? Do you have time?

Willst du mal mit mir einen Kaffee trinken gehen? – Do you want to go for coffee with me?

Sehr gerne, ich freue mich darauf – Gladly. I look forward to it.

Möchtest du vielleicht mal, etwas mit mir essen gehen. Ich kenne ein schönes Restaurant – Would you like to get something to eat with me? I know a nice restaurant.

Hast du Lust auf ein schönes Abendessen mit mir? – Do you fancy a nice dinner with me?

Wir könnten irgendwo mal schön essen gehen. Was hältst du von italienischem Essen? – We could go out to eat somewhere nice. What do you think about Italian food?

Ja, sehr gerne. Ich liebe italienische Küche. Kennst du ein schönes Restaurant? – Yes, very much. I love Italian cuisine. Do you know a nice restaurant?

Magst du Filme. Wenn ja, dann könnten wir mal ins Kino gehen? Was hältst du davon? – Do you like movies? If so, could we go to the movies? What do you think about it?

Ich liebe Filme. Gerne würde ich den neuen Film mit Johnny Depp sehen – I love movies. I would like to see the new movie with Johnny Depp.

Das klingt gut. Ich würde sehr gerne mal ausgehen – That sounds good. I would really like to go out sometime.

Liebend gern! – I would love to!

Tut mir leid, ich kann nicht. Ich habe viel zu tun – I am sorry, I can not. I have a lot to do.

Ich habe keine Zeit. Vielleicht ein anderes Mal – I have no time. Maybe another time.

Tut mir leid, aber du bist nicht mein Typ! – I am sorry, but you are not my type!

Gerne, möchtest du meine Nummer aufschreiben? – Gladly, would you like to write down my number?

Wie lautet deine Telefonnummer? – What is your phone number?

Kann ich deine Telefonnummer haben? – Could I take your phone number?

Kann ich deinen Facebooknamen haben? – Can I have your Facebook?

Würdest du mir deinen Instagram-Namen sagen? – Would you tell me your Instagram name?

Wie ist dein Nachname? – What is your last name?

You may also be in some situations where you want to give or receive compliments. Whatever the situation, you should be prepared with the right phrases:

Ich habe dich gleich bemerkt. Du siehst toll aus – I noticed you right away. You look great.

Du siehst sehr hübsch aus heute Abend. Ich mag deine Haare – You look very nice tonight. I like your hair.

Mir gefällt sehr was du anhast. Du bist sehr stylisch – I really like what you are wearing. You are very fashionable.

Mir gefällt dein Stil. Deine Jacke ist cool – I like your style. Your jacket is cool.

Du bist wunderschön (to the ladies). Ich finde du hast schöne Augen – You are beautiful (to the ladies). I think you have pretty eyes.

Du siehst wirklich klasse aus. Ich finde du bist sehr charmant – You are really good looking. I think you are very charming.

Du bist sehr attraktiv. Ich bin verzaubert – You are very attractive. I am enchanted.

Du hast wunderschöne Augen. Deine Augen strahlen – You have beautiful eyes. Your eyes are shining.

Du hast ein schönes Lächeln – You have a beautiful smile.

Danke für das Kompliment! – Thanks for the compliment!

Vielen Dank. Ich finde dich auch sehr toll – Many thanks. I think you are great too.

Dankeschön. Ich finde dich auch sehr stylisch. Mir gefällt dein T-shirt – Thank you. I think you are also very fashionable. I like your T-shirt.

Wie findest du den Ort hier? Gefällt es dir hier? – How do you like the place? Do you like it here?

Ich finde es nett. Das Essen ist gut – I think it is nice. The food is good.

Es ist nicht schlecht. Aber mir ein bisschen zu laut – It is not bad. But a bit too loud for me.

Sollen wir woanders hingehen? – Shall we go somewhere else?

Wenn es dir hier nicht gefällt, dann können wir gerne zu einem anderen Café gehen – If you do not like it here, we can go to another café.

Ich kenne einen guten Club. Wir können später dort hingehen – I know a good place. We can go there later.

Gerne. Das können wir machen – Gladly. We can do that.

Darf ich dich küssen? – Can I kiss you?

Würde es dich stören, wenn ich dich umarme? – Would it bother you if I hugged you?

Nein, das kannst du gerne machen – No, you can do it.

Das würde mir nicht gefallen. Sorry – I would not like that. Sorry.

Nein, danke – No, thanks.

Darf ich dich nach Hause begleiten? – Can I walk you home?

Kann ich dich nach Hause fahren? – Can I drive you home?

Ja, das wäre super. Du kannst mich gerne begleiten/fahren – Yes, that would be great. You can accompany me/drive.

Nein, danke. Ich werde ein Taxi nehmen – No, thanks. I will take a taxi.

Möchtest du noch auf einen Kaffee mit reinkommen? – Would you like to come in for a coffee?

Ich habe guten Wein Zuhause. Möchtest du noch reinkommen? – I have good wine at home. Do you still want to come in?

Möchtest du mit zu mir kommen? – Would you like to come back to mine?

Ja, gerne – Yes, gladly.

Nein, danke. Ich muss jetzt wirklich nach Hause gehen. Aber ich hatte viel Spaß und würde gerne wieder mit dir ausgehen – No, thanks. I really have to go home now. But I had a lot of fun and would like to go out with you again.

Danke, ich hatte einen wunderbaren Abend. Danke für das Abendessen – Thanks, I had a wonderful evening. Thank you for the dinner.

Ich würde dich gerne mal wiedersehen. Wann hast du wieder Zeit? – I would like to see you again. When will you have time again?

Ich bin mir nicht sicher. Ruf mich doch einfach mal an! – I am not sure. Just call me!

Ich ruf dich an. Gibst du mir deine Nummer? – I will call you. Would you give me your number?

Ja, sicher. Meine Nummer ist. – Yes, of course. My number is…

Ich hatte viel Spaß. Du bist sehr nett, aber ich muss jetzt gehen – I had a lot of fun. You are very nice, but I need to go now.

Ich muss leider gehen. Vielen Dank für alles – Unfortunately, I need to go. Thanks for everything.

Sometimes you will be in a situation where you will talk about emotions and if you like someone or not. You should know the following phrases:

Wie sind deine Gefühle gegenüber mir? – How are your feelings towards me?

Wie findest du mich? – What do you think of me?

Wie fandest du unser Date? – How did you like our date?

Ich finde dich toll. Die Zeit mit dir macht mir sehr viel Spaß. Ich mag es, mit dir zusammen Zeit zu verbringen – I think you are great. The time with you is a lot of fun. I like spending time with you.

Ich finde dich sehr attraktiv und du siehst wirklich gut aus – I think you are very attractive and you look great.

Du bist sehr intelligent, und das finde ich sehr gut. Ich kann mit dir über alles sprechen. Wir haben vieles gemeinsam – You are very intelligent, and I like that very much. I can talk to you about everything. We have a lot in common.

Möchtest du mein Freund/meine Freundin sein? – Do you want to be my boyfriend/girlfriend?

Du bist sehr nett, aber ich finde, dass wir einfach nicht zusammen passen – You are very nice, but I think we just do not fit together.

Ich hoffe du verstehst das nicht falsch, aber du bist nicht mein Typ. Danke für das schöne Date. Ich muss aber ablehnen – I hope you do not get it wrong, but you are not my type. Thanks for the nice date. But I have to refuse.

Ich fand den Abend toll, aber ich bin gerade nicht bereit für eine Beziehung. Können wir vielleicht erstmal Freunde sein? – I loved the evening, but I am just not ready for a relationship. Can we maybe be friends first?

Ich brauche noch ein bisschen Zeit zum Nachdenken. Kann ich dir in den nächsten Tagen Bescheid geben? – I need some time to think. Can I let you know in the next few days?

And here are some simple phrases to be straight forward when it comes to your feelings.

If you like the person you met and have gone on a date with, you can say:

Ich mag dich – I like you.

If those feelings are a little stronger, you can say:

Ich mag dich sehr – I like you a lot.

Ich bin in dich verliebt – I am in love with you.

When you are crazy about this person and want them to know, say:

Ich bin verrückt nach dir – I am crazy about you

If you are already in a relationship or deeply love the person, say:

Ich liebe dich! – I love you!

When it comes to proposing, then you simply say:

Willst du mich heiraten? – Will you marry me?

Ich möchte dich bis zum Ende meines Lebens lieben und mit dir zusammen sein. Willst du meine Frau werden? – I want to love you and be with you until the end of my life. Do you want to be my wife?

Du hast mein Leben zum Besseren verändert. Ich kann nicht mehr ohne dich – You have changed my life for the better. I cannot live without you.

When missing someone, you can tell the person:

Ich vermisse dich – I miss you

And when you see the person and want to tell her or him that you have missed them, you can say:

Ich habe dich vermisst – I have missed you

Ich bin schon seit Langem in dich verliebt und möchte, dass du das weißt – I have been in love with you for a long time and want you to know that.

Was fühlst du bei mir? Möchtest du mit mir zusammen sein? – How do you feel about me? Do you want to be with me?

Ich habe ein Geschenk für dich. Ich hoffe dass es dir gefallen wird – I have a present for you. I hope you will like it.

There are also situations where you need to express your sexual orientation or where other people will express that.

You should know the following phrases:

Ich bin heterosexuell – I am straight.

Ich bin schwul, lesbisch – I am gay.

Ich bin bisexuell – I am bisexual.

Let's now take a look at the important verbs and some new things we saw from the phrases:

tanzen – to dance

essen – to eat

spazieren gehen – to go for a walk

besuchen – to visit

besichtigen – to see

joggen – to jog

lesen – to read

mögen – to like

sich erholen – to relax

faulenzen – to be lazy

unternehmen – to do

reiten – to ride

segeln – to sail

singen – to singkegeln – to bowl

grillen – to grill

sich beschäftigen – to be occupied with something

schwimmen – to swim

reisen – to travel

finden – to find

angeln – to fish

einkaufen gehen – to go shopping

verbringen – to spend time

Rad fahren – to ride the bike

Ski fahren – to ski

einkaufen gehen – to go shop

Gittare spielen – to play the guitar

Musik hören – to listen to music

We will now go over the conjugation of some verbs.

Tanzen is being conjugated regularly. However, it is not the same with "essen". Essen is a verb where you will need to remember the conjugation and learn it separately. This verb changes its form in the second and third person singular and the second person plural.

Ess + en

Ich esse

Du isst

Er, sie, es isst

Wir essen

Ihr isst

Sie essen

In the German language, most verbs end with "-en", (lachen, laufen, machen...). The basic form of a verb, i.e., the non-conjugated form of a verb, is called the "infinitive". Verbs in the dictionary are always in the infinitive. Under certain conditions, an "infinitive" may also be in the sentence. This is often the case if there are two verbs in the same sentence. As a verb form, the infinitive can be in the sentence with or without "zu" (to).

Infinitiv without "zu": Ich kann die Prüfung schaffen. I can pass the exam.

Infinitiv with "zu": Ich hoffe, die Prüfung zu schaffen. I hope to pass the exam.

In the following cases, the infinitive sentence is formed without "zu":

When using the modal verbs:

What are MODAL VERBS?

There are a total of six modal verbs: "können", "wollen", "möchten", "sollen", "müssen", "dürfen" (can, want, want, should, must, may).

With modal verbs, you change the content of a statement but not the plot—because it makes a difference if someone has to do something or must do something.

Modal verbs usually stand with a second verb (the "full verb") and need to be conjugated.

Examples

Ich kann kein Deutsch sprechen – I cannot speak German.

Ich darf kein Gitarre spielen – I may not play the guitar.

Ich muss heute nicht lernen – I do not have to learn today.

Ich möchte heute lernen – I want to learn today.

Wir sollen zur Schule gehen – We should go to school.

Word order

Modal verbs are almost always used with a second verb (the full verb). The full verb then goes to the end of the sentence, and the modal verb is conjugated and thus takes the second or first position.

Particularities:

If the main verb is obvious and results from the situation, it is often omitted in colloquial language.

Kannst du Deutsch (sprechen)? – Can you speak (German)?

Ich will ein Wasser (trinken) – I want (to drink) a water.

We also don't need "zu" when we use the verbs " bleiben" (to stay) and " lassen" (to let).

Sie bleibt gerne im Bett liegen – She stays to lay in the bed.

Ich lasse den Hund spielen – I let the dog play.

Also when using the verbs "gehen" and "fahren", "sehen" and "hören".

Jeden Samstag gehen meine Eltern in der Stadt einkaufen – Every Saturday my parents go to shop in the city.

Meine Mutter fährt gerne mit ihrem Auto – My mother likes to drive her car.

Man sieht viele Vögel fliegen – Many birds can be seen flying.

Ich höre die Vögel zwitschern – I hear the birds chirping.

There are a number of fixed verb combinations that are formed according to this pattern:

arbeiten gehen – to go to work

einkaufen gehen – to go to shop

spazieren gehen – to go for a walk

angeln gehen – to go to fish

schwimmen gehen – to go to swim

schlafen gehen – to go to sleep

Let's do the conjugation:

spazieren gehen – to go for a walk

Ich gehe spazieren

Du gehst spazieren

Er, sie, es geht spazieren

Wir gehen spazieren

Ihr geht spazieren

Sie gehen spazieren

As you can see, the verb "spazieren" is always in the infinitive, and the verb "gehen" is being conjugated regularly.

"Besuchen", "besichtigen", and "joggen" are conjugated normally.

"lesen" is a little different:

Ich lese

Du liest

Er, sie, es liest

Wir lesen

Ihr liest

Sie lesen

"mögen" is also different:

 ich mag – I like

du magst – you like

er, sie, es mag – he, she, it likes

wir mögen – we like

ihr mögt – you like

sie mögen – They like

Ich mag dich – I like you.

Magst du Fußball? – Do you like football?

Mögt ihr Deutsch? – Do you like German?

mögen + Nomen = mögen + nouns

gern + Aktivität = gern + activity

Ich mag Fußball – I like football.

Ich will Fußball spielen – I want to play football.

Ich spiele gern Fußball – I like playing football. ("gern" is used for activities)

Ich mag Deutsch – I like German.

Ich lerne gern Deutsch – I like learning German.

"Erholen" and "faulenzen" are conjugated normally.

"Unternehmen" is conjugated like "nehmen" (ich unternehme, du unternimmst…)

And all other verbs from the list are conjugated regularly.

Let's go over these verbs with nouns:

Besides verbs with prefixes, there is another group treated like the separable verbs, the so-called compound verbs. In this group, a verb joins another and gets a new meaning.

Adjective + verb (we will get to this group soon)

Noun + Verb

Verb + verb (we discussed this just now (spazieren gehen, zwitschern hören)

Here are the examples for **Noun + Verb:**

Rad fahren – to ride the bike

Ich fahre gerne Rad – I like to ride the bike.

Ski fahren – to ski

Ich fahre Ski – I ski.

Gittare spielen – to play the guitar

Ich spiele gerne Gittare – I like to play the guitar.

Musik hören – to listen to music

In most cases, the noun takes the last position in the sentence, and the verb is in the first or second place.

Conjugation:

Ich fahre Ski

Du fährst Ski

Er, sie, es fährt Ski

Wir fahren Ski

Ihr fahrt Ski

Sie fahren Ski

We covered the important verbs and conjugation, so now it is time to talk about another word group: "ADJECTIVES".

Here are some examples: schön (beautiful), interessant (interesting), gut (good), langweilig (boring), and gern (gladly).

The adjective (= property word) is a companion to the noun that specifies it. It can either be in front of the noun or after the verb of the sentence. If it stands before the noun, one uses it attributively; if it stands after the verb, it is predicative.

Adjectives—such as nouns, pronouns, and articles—can be declined so that they can be matched in number and case. In their gender, however, they are the same. It is also important to use them with a definite or indefinite article.

Adjectives with a definite article

Singular (masculine)

N der **kleine** Hund (the **small** dog)

G des kleines Hundes

D dem kleinen Hund

A den kleinen Hund

Singular (feminine)

N die **schöne** Blume (the **beautiful** flower)

G der schönen Blume

D der schönen Blume

A die schöne Blume

Singular (neutral)

N das **alte** Buch (the **old** book)

G des alten Buches

D dem alten Buch

A das alte Buch

Plural (masculine)

N die **kleinen** Hunde (the **small** dogs)

G der kleinen Hunde

D den kleinen Hunden

A die kleinen Hunde

Plural (feminine)

N die **schönen** Blumen (the **beautiful** flowers)

G der schönen Blumen

D den schönen Blumen

A die schönen Blumen

Plural (neutral)

N die **alten** Bücher (the **old** books)

G der alten Bücher

D den alten Büchern

A die alten Bücher

Example

Das schöne Mädchen verkauft **guten Saft** – The beautiful girl sells good juice.

Adjectives with a indefinite article

Singular (masculine)

N ein **kleiner** Hund (a **small** dog)

G eines kleinen Hundes

D einem kleinen Hund

A einen kleinen Hund

Da ist ein kleiner Hund – There is a little dog.

Singular (feminine)

N eine **schöne** Blume (a **beautiful** flower)

G einer schönen Blume

D einer schönen Blume

A eine schöne Blume

Ich kaufe dir eine schöne Blume – I am buying a nice flower for you.

Singular (neutral)

N ein **altes** Buch (a **old** book)

G eines alten Buches

D einem alten Buch

A ein altes Buch

Ich habe es in einem alten Buch gelesen – I have read it in an old book.

Plural (masculine)

N **kleine** Hunde (**small** dogs)

G kleiner Hunde

D kleinen Hunden

A kleine Hunde

Plural (feminine)

N **schöne** Blumen (**beautiful** flowers)

G schöner Blumen

D schönen Blumen

A schöne Blumen

Plural (neutral)

N **alte** Bücher (**old** books)

G alter Bücher

D alten Büchern

A alte Bücher

STRONG AND WEAK DECLINATION

The declination of a property word can be weak or strong. An adjective is weakly declined if another companion with the corresponding endings determines the declination of the noun. Otherwise, the adjective is strongly declined.

Examples of weak and strong declension:

Weak Declination – Strong Declination

die starken Männer – starke Männer

Ich habe die starken Männer gesehen./ Das sind starke Männer – I have seen the strong men. These are strong men.

der heiße Kaffee – heißer Kaffee

Ich finde der heiße Kaffee schmeckt gut/Das ist heißer Kaffee – I think the hot coffee tastes good/That is hot coffee.

das helle Licht – helles Licht

Siehst du das helle Licht?/Ich sehe helles Licht – Do you see the bright light?/I see bright light.

mit dem frischen Obst – mit frischem Obst

Ich nehme die Schüssel mit dem frischen Obst/Ich mag den Nachtisch mit frischem Obst – I take the bowl of fresh fruit/I like the dessert with fresh fruit.

auf der nassen Erde – auf nasser Erde

Auf der nassen Erde ist es schmutzig/Ich laufe auf nasser Erde – It is dirty on the wet ground/I walk on wet ground.

in der kalten Luft – in kalter Luft

In der kalten Luft, kann man sich erkälten/Ich spaziere in kalter Luft – In the cold air, you can catch a cold/I walk in the cold air.

Adjectives can be in POSITIVE, COMPARATIVE or SUPERLATIVE.

In the comparative, the adjectives have the ending "-er"; in the superlative, they have "am" and the ending "-sten" is given.

Positive (+), Comparative (++), Superlative (+++)

Klein, kleiner, am kleinsten (small, smaller, the smallest).

Der Hund ist klein. Die Katze ist kleiner. Die Maus ist am kleinsten.

The dog is small. The cat is smaller. The mouse is the smallest.

Schön, schöner, am schönsten (beautiful, more beautiful, the most beautiful).

Ihre Tasche ist schön. Ihre Brieftasche ist schöner. Ihre Jacke ist am schönsten.

Her bag is beautiful. Her wallet is more beautiful. Her jacket is the most beautiful.

Einfach, einfacher, am einfachsten (easy, easier, the easiest).

Die erste Aufgabe ist einfach. Die zweite Aufgabe ist einfacher. Die letzte Aufgabe ist am einfachsten. The first task is easy. The second task is easier. The last task is the easiest.

The short adjectives that have an "-a-", "-o-", or "-u" get an umlaut in the comparative and superlative.

Positive (+), Comparative (++), Superlative (+++)

Lang, länger, am längsten (long, longer, the longest).

Die Haare sind lang. Die Beine sind Länger. Der Körper ist am längsten.

The hair is long. The legs are longer. The body is the longest.

Jung, jünger, am jüngsten (young, younger, the youngest).

Mein Bruder ist jung. Meine Schwester ist jünger. Ich bin am jüngsten.

My brother is young. My sister is younger. I am the youngest.

Grob, gröber, am gröbsten (coarse, coarser, coarsest).

Mein Opa ist grob. Mein Bruder ist gröber. Mein Vater ist am gröbsten.

My grandpa is coarse. My brother is coarser. My dad is the coarsest.

Adjectives that end in "-t", "-d", "-tz", "-z", "-s", "-ss", "-sch"or "-ß" get the ending "-este" in the superlative.

Positive (+), Comparative (++), Superlative (+++)

Wild, wilder, am wildesten (wild, wilder, the wildest).

Der Hase ist wild. Der Bär ist wilder. Der Löwe ist am wildesten.

The rabbit is wild. The bear is wilder. The lion is the wildest.

Kalt, kälter, am kältesten (cold, colder, the coldest).

Gestern war es kalt. Heute ist es kälter. Morgen wird es am kältesten sein.

Yesterday it was cold. Today it is colder. Tomorrow will be the coldest.

Hart, härter, am härtesten (hard, harder, the hardest).

Biologie ist hart. Physik ist härter. Mathe ist am härtesten.

Biology is hard. Physics is harder. Math is the hardest.

Adjectives ending in "-el" or "-er" lose the "-e-" in the comparative.

Positive (+), Comparative (++), Superlative (+++)

Dunkel, dunkler, am dunkelsten (dark, darker, the darkest).

Am Nachmittag wird es dunkel. Am Abend wird es dunkler. In der Nacht ist es am dunkelsten.

It gets dark in the afternoon. In the evening it gets darker. It is darkest at night.

Teuer, teurer, am teuersten (expensive, more expensive, the most expensive).

Das Kleid ist teuer. Der Ring ist teurer. Das Auto ist am teuersten.

The dress is expensive. The ring is more expensive. The car is the most expensive.

Irregular forms:

Positive (+), Comparative (++), Superlative (+++)

Gut, besser, am besten (good, better, the best).

Das Sandwich ist gut. Der Kuchen ist besser. Die Pizza ist am besten.

The sandwich is good. The cake is better. The pizza is best.

Viel, mehr, am meisten (much, more, most).

Ich esse viel. Sie isst mehr. Er isst am meisten.

I eat a lot. She eats more. He eats the most.

Gern, lieber, am liebsten (like, like more, like most).

Ich habe meine Freunde gern. Ich mag meine Cousine lieber. Ich mag meine Schwester am liebsten.

I like my friends. I like my cousin more. I like my sister the most.

Hoch, höher, am höchsten (high, higher, the highest).

Das Haus ist hoch. Das Gebäude ist höher. Der Wolkenkratzer ist am höchsten.

The house is high. The building is higher. The skyscraper is highest.

Nah, näher, am nächsten (close, closer, the closest).

Du bist mir nah. Er ist mir näher. Sie ist mir am nächsten.

You are close to me. He is closer to me. She is closest to me.

Groß, größer, am größten (big, bigger, the biggest).

Das Buch ist groß. Das Zimmer ist größer. Die Wohnung ist am größten.

The book is big. The room is bigger. The apartment is the biggest.

Oft, öfter, am häufigsten (often, more often, most often).

Ich gehe zum Arzt oft. Ich gehe ins Kino öfter. Ich gehe ins Einkaufszentrum am häufigsten.

I go to the doctor often. I go to the cinema more often. I go to the mall most often.

When we want to compare something, we say:

so + Positive + wie

Er ist fast so alt wie sie – He is almost as old as she.

Er ist genauso schön wie Jonas – He is just as beautiful as Jonas.

Comparativ + als

Er ist älter als seine Schwester – He is older than his sister.

Das Haus ist schöner als die Wohnung – The house is more beautiful than the apartment.

Here are some words and phrases you can use to **describe the look and personality of someone**, as well as some words for **different emotions**.

When you want to describe physical characteristics, then you can use the following adjectives:

Groß – Tall

Er ist sehr groß – He is very tall.

Klein – short/small

Sie ist klein – She is short.

Das Kleid ist klein – The dress is small.

Schlank – slim

Du bist wirklich schlank – You are really slim.

Dünn – thin

Die Jacke ist ziemlich dünn – The jacket is pretty thin.

Dick – fat

Mein Bruder war früher dick – My brother was fat before.

Übergewichtig – obese

Bin ich übergewichtig? – Am I obese?

gut gebaut – well built

Der Mann ist gut gebaut – The man is well built.

Übergewichtig – overweight

Meine Mutter ist übergewichtig – My mother is overweight.

Mittelgroß – medium size

Die Tasche ist mittelgroß – The bag is medium size.

gut gekleidet, gut angezogen – well dressed

Meine Schwester ist immer gut gekleidet – My sister is always well dressed.

klug – smart

Meine Eltern sind sehr klug – My parents are very smart.

ungepflegt – scruffy

Seine Haare sind ungepflegt – His hair is scruffy.

gut aussehend – good looking

Sie ist gut assehend – She is good looking.

Attraktiv – attractive

Die Wohnung ist attraktiv – The apartment is attractive.

Schön – beautiful

Mein Bruder ist schön – My brother is beautiful.

Hübsch – pretty

Das Hemd ist hübsch – The shirt is pretty.

attraktiv – handsome

Mark ist sehr attraktiv – Mark is very handsome.

Hässlich – ugly

Das Haus ist hässlich – The house is ugly.

Alt – old

Das Buch ist sehr alt – The book is very old.

Jung – young

Meine Cousine ist sehr jung – My cousin is very young.

mittleren Alters – middle-aged

Ich habe Eltern mittleren Alters – I have parents that are middle-aged.

Glatzköpfig – bald

Mein Onkel ist glatzköpfig – My uncle is bald.

Glatzköpfig – baldheaded

Bart – beard

Ich möchte einen Bart – I want a beard.

Schnurrbart – mustache

Er hat einen Schnurrbart – He has a mustache.

langes Haar – long hair

Alle in meiner Familie haben langes Haar – Everyone in my family has long hair.

kurzes Haar – short hair

Ich mag kurzes Haar – I like short hair.

glattes Haar – straight hair

Sie hatte glattes Haar – She had straight hair.

Locken – curly hair

Sie hat sehr schöne Locken – She has beautiful curly hair.

Blond – fair-haired

Meine Mutter ist blond – My mother is fair-haired.

Braunhaarig – brown-haired

Meine Schwester ist braunhaarig – My sister is brown-haired.

Dunkelhaarig – dark-haired

Mein Freund ist dunkelhaarig – My friend is dark-haired.

Rothaarig – ginger-haired

Er ist rothaarig – He is ginger-haired.

Blondine – blond

Sie ist eine Blondine – She is blonde.

Brünette – brunette

Sie ist eine Brünette – She is a brunette.

Rothaariger, Rothaarige – redhead

Er ist ein Rothaariger – He is a redhead.

When you are feeling a certain way, then you can express that by saying the following phrases:

Froh – happy

Wegen den kleinen Dingen bin ich froh – I am happy because of the small things.

Traurig – sad

Das hat mich sehr traurig gemacht – This makes me very sad.

Miserabel – miserable

Sie ist sehr missmutig – I am very miserable.

Besorgt – worried

Warum bist du besorgt? – Why are you worried?

Depremiert – depressed

Ich bin heute deprimiert – I am depressed today.

Aufgeregt – excited

Ich bin so aufgeregt wegen der Party – I am so excited because of the party.

Gelangweilt – bored

Ich bin im Unterricht gelangweilt – I am bored in class.

Genervt – fed up

Sie ist wegen ihm genervt – She is fed up because of him.

Erfreut – pleased

Ich bin sehr erfreut – I am very pleased.

Entzückt – delighted

Ich bin entzückt – I am delighted.

Überrascht – surprised

Meine Mutter hat mich überrascht – My mother surprised me.

Erstaunt – astonished

Dieses Haus hat mich erstaunt – I am astonished by the house.

Enttäuscht – disappointed

Meine Freunde haben mich enttäuscht – My friends have disappointed me.

Begeistert – excited

Davon bin ich begeistert – I am excited because of that.

Entspannt – relaxed

Er ist sehr entspannt – He is very relaxed.

Gestresst – stressed

Sei nicht gestresst – Do not be stressed.

Ängstlich – anxious

Ich bin wegen der Fahrt ängstlich – I am anxious because of the ride.

Müde – tired

Wegen meiner Reise bin ich jetzt müde – I am tired because of my trip.

Erschöpft – exhausted

Meine Tante ist erschöpft – My aunt is exhausted.

Verärgert – annoyed

Mein Bruder ist verärgert – My brother is annoyed.

Wütend – angry

Bist du auf mich wütend? – Are you angry?

Lebending – livid

Die Natur ist so lebendig – The nature is so alive.

Angeekelt – disgusted

Ich bin angeekelt – I am disgusted.

When you want to describe a personality, then you can use the following phrases:

Zuversichtlich – confident

Ich war schon immer zuversichtlich – I was always confident.

Sensibel – sensitive

Meine Schwester ist sehr sensibel – My sister is very sensitive.

Ruhig – calm

Er ist ruhig – He is calm

Hitzköpfig – hotheaded

Warum bist du so hitzköpfig? – Why are you so hotheaded?

Impulsiv – impulsive

Du bist viel zu impulsiv – You are too impulsive.

Fröhlich – cheerful

Sei einfach fröhlich – Just be cheerful.

Großzügig – generous

Diese Tat war sehr großzügig – This act was very generous.

Nett – kind

Du bist sehr nett – You are very kind.

Gemein – mean

Das war gemein –This was mean.

Verrückt – crazy

Die Frau ist doch verrückt – The woman is crazy.

Ernst – serious

Das Gespräch ist ernst – The talk is serious.

Ehrlich – honest

Sei ehrlich zu dir selbst – Be honest to yourself.

Unehrlich – dishonest

Er war unehrlich – He was dishonest.

gut gelaunt – good-humored

Sie ist immer gut gelaunt – She is always good-humored.

schlecht gelaunt – bad-tempered

Ihre Schwester is schlecht gelaunt – Her sister is bad-tempered.

Launisch – moody

Warum bist du launig? – Why are you moody?

Fleißig – hardworking

Sie ist sehr fleißig. – She is very hardworking.

Faul – lazy

Mein Hund ist faul – My dog is lazy.

Schlau – clever

Meine Schwester war schon immer schlau – My sister was always very clever.

Intelligent – intelligent

Einige Menschen sind einfach von Natur aus intelligent – Some people are just naturally intelligent.

Unintelligent – unintelligent

Du bist sehr unintelligent – You are very unintelligent.

Arrogant – arrogant

Sei doch nicht so arrogant – Do not be so arrogant.

Hochnäsig – snobbish

Sie ist sehr hochnäsig – She is very snobbish.

Glücklich – happy

Ich bin mit mir selbst zufrieden – I am happy with myself.

Unglücklich – unhappy

Wegen des Spiels bin ich sehr unglücklich – I am very unhappy because of the game.

Dumm – stupid

Regeln sind dumm – Rules are stupid.

Extrovertiert – outgoing

Der Junge ist sehr extrovertiert – The boy is very outgoing.

Vorsichtig – cautious

Sie ist immer vorsichtig – She is always cautious.

Abenteuerlustig – adventurous

Meine Freunde sind abenteuerlustig – My friends are adventurous.

Schüchtern – shy

Sei nicht so schüchtern – Do not be so shy.

Introvertiert – introverted

Manchmal bin ich introvertiert – I am sometimes introverted.

Extrovertiert – extroverted

Aber bei Partys bin ich extrovertiert – But I am extroverted at parties.

Unbeschwert – easygoing

Er ist unbeschwert – He is easygoing.

Grob – rude

Der Polizist ist grob – The policeman is rude.

schlecht erzogen, ohne Manieren – bad-mannered

Ihre Kinder sind schlecht erzogen – Her children are bad-mannered.

Unhöflich – impolite

Der Kellner ist unhöflich – The waiter is impolite.

Emotional – emotional

Der Film war emotional – The movie was emotional.

Höflich – polite

Die Frau ist wirklich höflich – The woman is really polite.

Lustig – funny

Der Witz war lustig – The joke was funny.

Witzig – witty

Der ist aber witzig – He is witty.

Langweilig – boring

Warum bist du so langweilig? – Why are you so boring?

Geduldig – patient

Sie ist immer geduldig – She is always patient.

Ungeduldig – impatient

Ihr Bruder ist aber ungeduldig – Her brother is impatient.

Gebildet – sophisticated

Die Lehrerin is gebildet – The teacher is sophisticated.

Frech – cheeky

Sei nicht frech! – Do not be cheeky!

Freundlich – friendly

Alle waren sehr freundlich – Everyone was friendly.

Unfreundlich – unfriendly

Die Kinder sind unfreundlich – The kids are unfriendly.

Eingebildet – conceited

Sein Freund ist eingebildet – His friend is conceited.

Bescheiden – modest

Sie leben bescheiden – They live modest.

Tapfer – brave

Der Junge ist echt tapfer – The boy is really brave.

Ängstlich – cowardly

Der Mann ist ängstlich – The man is cowardly.

Zerstreut – absent-minded

Die Klasse ist zerstreut – The class is absent-minded.

Talentiert – talented

Das Mädchen ist talentiert – The girl is talented.

Gehorsam/brav – obedient

Sei brav! – Be obedient!

Ungehorsam – disobedient

Die Kinder sind ungehorsam – The children are disobedient.

Prinzipientreu – principled

Sie ist prinzipientrue – She is principled.

Korrupt – corrupt

Der ist korrupt – He is corrupt.

Skrupellos – unscrupulous

Wie skrupellos! – How unscrupulous.

You can use adjectives in many situations. Try to practice by yourself or with someone. Describe someone with as many adjectives from the list and make sure you use them correctly. Also form sentences with the positive, comparative or superlative.

Let's move on!

Chapter 7 – Food and Drink

Quick Overview

- Vocabulary
- Phrases for the grocery store, market, restaurant or when eating at a friend's house
- Prepositions

Now it is time to go over different types of food and drinks and how you can shop for the things you need or ask for something in a restaurant. You will also learn to order a meal and pay for it. However, just like any other topic, this one requires knowledge of the main vocabulary.

im Lebensmittelgeschäft – in the grocery store

in der Bäckerei – in the backery

im Supermarkt – in the supermarket

in der Fleischerei – in the butchery

in der Konditorei – in the pastry shop

auf dem Markt – on the market

die Lebensmittel – groceries

das Brot – bread

die Semmel – roll

die Brezel – pretzel

der Kuchen – cake

die Torte – pie

die Butter – butter

das Öl – oil

die Milch – milk

der Joghurt – yogurt

das Ei – egg

das Mehl – flour

der Zucker – sugar

der Käse – cheese

die Wurst – sausage

die Nudeln – pasta

der Reis – rice

das Eis – ice

die Schokolade – chocolate

das Bonbon – bonbon

das Kaugummi – chewing gum

die Marmelade – jam

der Honig – honey

die Suppe – soup

die Pommes Frites – fries

der Hamburger – hamburger

das Kotelett – chop

das Schnitzel – Schnitzel

das Faschierte – minced meat

das Rindfleisch – beef meat

das Kalbfleisch – calf meat

das Schaffleisch – sheep meat

das Lammfleisch – lamb meat

das Huhn / Hühnchen – chicken meat

das Schweinefleisch – pork

der Fisch – fish

die Ziege – goat

der Aufstrich – spread

der Sauerrahm – sour cream

die Schlagsahne – whipped cream

das Ketchup – ketchup

die Mayonnaise – mayonnaise

der Senf – mustard

Das Obst (die Früchte) – fruit

der Apfel – apple

die Birne – pear

die Banane – banana

die Zitrone – lemon

der Granatapfel – pomegranate

der Pfirsich – peach

die Orange – orange

die Mandarine – mandarine

die Kiwi – kiwi

die Weintraube – grapes

die Ananas – pineapple

die Erdbeere – strawberry

die Himbeere – raspberry

die Brombeere – blackberry

die Kirsche – cherry

die Wassermelone – watermelon

die Grapefruit – grapefruit

die Pflaume – plum

die Mango – mango

die Feige – fig

das Gemüse – vegetables

die Tomate – tomato

die Gurke – cucumber

die Paprika – paprika

 die Pepperoni – pepperoni

die Karotte – carrot

die Zwiebel – onion

der Knoblauch – garlic

die Zucchini – zucchini

die Bohne – bean

die Erbse – pea

die Linsen – lentils

der Mais – corn

der Chicoree – chicory

das Kraut – herb

der Kohl – cabbage

die Kartoffel – potato

der Porree/Lauch – leek

das Radieschen – radish

der Pilz – mushroom

die Avocado – avocado

die Artischocke – artichocke

der Broccoli – broccoli

der Kürbis – pumpkin

die Olive – olive

der grüne Salat – green salad

der Blumenkohl – cauliflower

der Radicchio – radicchio

der Chinakohl – Chinese cabbage

der Spargel – asparagus

die Sellerie – celery

die Kräuter – herbs

die Petersilie – parsley

der Schnittlauch – chives

der Oregano – oregano

der Thymian – thyme

der Basilikum – basil

der Lorbeer – laurel

die Minze – mint

der Rosmarin – rosemary

der Dill – dill

Getränke – drinks

das Wasser – water

der Saft – juice

der Tee – tea

der Kaffee – coffee

die Limonade – lemonade

das Sprudelwasser – sparkling water

der Milchshake – milkshake

die heiße Schokolade – hot chocolate

der Kakao – cocoa

der Espresso – espresso

der Alkohol – alcohol

der Wein – wine

der Weißwein – white wine

der Rotwein – red wine

das Bier – beer

der Likör – liqueur

die Küche – kitchen

das Backblech – baking tray

die Backform – baking mold

der Topf – pot

die Kasserolle – casserole

das Sieb – sieve

die Pfanne – pan

das Schneidbrett – cutting board

die Schüssel – bowl

die Tasse – cup

der Teller – plate

die Teekanne – teapot

der Wasserkessel – kettle

die Thermosflasche – thermos bottle

der Wasserkocher – water heater

das Besteck – cutlery

die Gabel – fork

das Küchenmesser – kitchen knife

der Löffel – spoon

das Messer – knife

das Geschirrtuch – tea towel

das Glas – glass

der Schöpflöffel – ladle

die Serviette – napkin

der Schwamm – sponge

die Knoblauchpresse – garlic press

die Küchenrolle – kitchen roll

der Salzstreuer – salt shaker

die Pfeffermühle – pepper mill

die Zuckerdose – sugarcan

der Toaster – toaster

die Kaffeemaschine – coffee machine

die Küchenmaschine – kitchen machine

der Schneebesen – whisk

die Mikrowelle – microwave

die Spüle – sink

der Herd – stove

das Backrohr – oven

der Mülleimer – trash can

der Kühlschrank – refrigerator

der Geschirrspüler – dishwasher

die Brotdose – breadcan

der Aschenbecher – ashtray

der Besen – broom

die Schaufel – shovel

die Alufolie – aluminium foil

der Dunstabzug – extractor hood

der Kochlöffel – cooking spoon

das Restaurant – restaurant

der Kellner – waiter

die Kellnerin – waitress

der Tisch – table

das Frühstück – breakfast

das Mittagessen – lunch

das Abendessen – dinner

das Dessert/ der Nachtisch – dessert

die Rechnung – bill

Since you know the most important vocabulary, let's continue with some phrases you could use when shopping for groceries or going to a market or restaurant.

If you are in the supermarket, the worker might ask you:

Kann ich Ihnen helfen? – Can I help you?

Or:

Was kann ich für Sie tun? – What can I do for you?

Then, if you need something specific, you can say:

Haben Sie Milch/Bananen/Erbsen? – Do you have milk/bananas/beans?

Ich möchte Kartoffeln – I want potatoes.

Ja, das haben wir! – Yes, we have that.

If you then want to ask for a certain amount of something, you can say:

Eine Dose Erbsen, bitte! – One can of beans, please!

Ich möchte ein Kilo Bananen, bitte! – I want one kilo of bananas, please!

When asking for the price, just say:

Was kostet ein Kilo Tomaten? – How much is one kilo of tomatoes?

Ein Kilo Tomaten kostet 2 Euro und 10 Cent – One kilo of tomatoes is 2 Euro and 10 Cents.

Ich möchte zwei Kilo, bitte! – I want two kilos, please!

If you need 500 grams or half a kilo, then you can say:

Ich brauche ein halbes Kilo Spinat – I need half a kilo of spinach.

Ich nehme 300 grams frischen Käse, vier Kilo Tomaten, und drei Stangen Sellerie – I will take 300 grams of fresh cheese, four kilos of tomatoes, and three stalks of celery.

Haben Sie Brot? – Do you have bread?

Nein, wir haben kein Brot – No, we do not have bread.

Möchten Sie sonst noch etwas? – Do you want something else?

Ich möchte ein Sechserpack Bier, bitte! – I want a six pack of beer, please!

Ist das alles? – Is that everything?

Ja, das ist alles – Yes, that is everything.

Wie viel macht das? – How much is that?

Das macht 10 Euro 20 Cent, bitte! – That would be 10 Euro and 20 cent, please!

Danke. Auf Wiedersehen! – Thank you. Goodbye.

Danke für Ihren Einkauf! Kommen Sie bald wieder! – Thank you for your purchase! Come again soon!

When you want to ask for the price, you simply say:

Was macht das?/Was kostet das? – How much is that?

Das macht (/kostet) 10 Euro und 20 Cent – That is 10 Euro and 20 cents.

When you are in the grocery store and need to find something, ask the worker:

Entschuldigung, wo sind denn hier die Tomaten? – Excuse me, where are the tomatoes?

Da vorne, in der Gemüseabteilung – There, in the vegetable section.

If you did look it up and couldn't find it, then say:

Da habe ich schon nachgeschaut, aber ich habe sie nicht gesehen – I have already looked there, but I didn't see them.

Doch, sie sind vorne links, gleich am Eingang – Yes, they are there in the front on the left side, just by the entrance.

Danke, ich geh nochmal nachsehen. – Thank you, I will go check again.

Ist irgendwas im Angebot? – Is there any offer?

Wir haben frischen Spargel; da kostet das Kilo nur 5 Euro – We have fresh asparagus; one kilo is just 5 Euro.

Ich brauche noch Kartoffeln – I also need potato.

Die sind dort drüben neben den Zwiebeln – They are there, next to the onions.

Dankeschön! – Thank you!

Möchten Sie einen Beutel? – Do you want a bag?

Ja, bitte! – Yes, please.

Hier noch die Rechnung – Here, the bill.

Im Gasthaus/im Restaurant – In the restaurant

When you want to go out to eat with your friends, you should know how to speak to the waiter and other staff at the restaurant. Try to memorize the following phrases:

Guten Tag, wir haben eine Reservierung – Good day, we have a reservation.

Wir haben einen Tisch reserviert – We have reserved a table.

Haben Sie einen Tisch für zwei/drei/vier Personen, bitte? – Do you have a table for two, three, four people, please?

Haben Sie einen Tisch reserviert? – Have you booked a table?

Ja, wir haben einen Tisch am Fenster und in der Ecke – Yes, we have a table by the window and in the corner.

Dann nehmen wir den Tisch bei dem Fenster bitte – Then we will take the table by the window, please.

Momentan, haben wir nichts frei. Aber ab 3 Uhr werden wir einen Tisch frei haben. Passt das? – Currently, we have nothing free. But from 3 o'clock there will be a free table. Is that fine?

Alles ist besetzt. Möchten Sie für morgen reservieren? – Everything is reserved. Would you like to book for tomorrow?

Ja, gerne. Ich möchte einen Tisch für 3 Personen reservieren. Haben Sie um etwas um circa 12 Uhr? – Yes, gladly. I would like to reserve a table for 3 people. Do you have something at 12 o'clock?

Guten Tag, möchten Sie bestellen? – Good day, would you like to order?

Wir möchten gern bestellen – We would like to order.

Bitte, was bekommen Sie? – Please, what would you like?

Was kann ich für Sie tun? – What can I do for you?

Ich stehe Ihnen zur Verfügung – I am at your disposal.

Wie viele sind Sie? – How many are you?

Folgen Sie mir, bitte – Would you follow me, please?

Hätten Sie gerne die Karte? – Would you like to see the menu?

Kann ich Ihre Bestellung aufnehmen, der Herr/die Dame? – Could I take your order, sir/madam?

Was hätten Sie gerne als Vorspeise? Kann ich Ihnen etwas anbieten? – What would you like as a starter? Can I recommend something?

Was möchten Sie gerne trinken? – What would you like to drink?/Anything to drink?

Was hätten Sie gerne als Hauptgericht/Dessert? – What would you like for main course/dessert?

Wie möchten Sie Ihr Steak? (kurz angebraten, in der Mitte noch rosa, durchgebraten) – How would you like your steak? (rare, medium, well done)

Wir haben sehr leckere Salate. Möchen Sie einen? – We have delicious salads to offer. Do you want one?

Möchten Sie auch Dressing dazu haben? – Do you want dressing with it?

Das Fleisch ist sehr gut. Dies ist das erste Mal, dass ich so etwas esse – The meat is very good. This is the first time I am eating something like this.

Entschuldigung, das Fleisch ist verdorben. Es riecht komisch – Excuse me, the meat is off. It smells weird.

Wie war das Essen. Hat es Ihnen geschmeckt? – How was the food? Did it taste good?

Bezahlen Sie zusammen? – Are you paying together?

Könnten Sie bitte noch etwas warten. Es wird gleich ein Tisch frei. Die Gäste bezahlen gerade – Can you please wait. There will be a free table right away. The guests are just paying.

Möchten Sie eine Beilage dazu? Wir haben gegrilltes Gemüse oder gebratene Kartoffeln – Would you like a side dish? We have grilled vegetables or fried potatoes

Möchten Sie vielleicht das Tagesgericht probieren? Es ist eine tolle Tomatensuppe und ein vegetarischer Burger – Would you maybe like to try the dish of the day? It is a great tomato soup and a veggie burger.

Wie lange müssen wir warten? – How long do we have to wait?

Es dauert circa 15 Minuten – It will take about 15 minutes.

Ist alles in Ordnung? – Is everything alright?

Guten Appetit! – Enjoy your meal!

Als Vorspeise, hätte ich gerne den griechischen Salat. Und als Hauptgericht möchte ich die Pizza, aber ohne Oliven, bitte – As an appetizer, I would like the Greek salad. And as a main course I want the pizza, but without olives, please.

Könnte ich bitte Gemüse anstelle von Reis haben? – Could I have vegetables instead of the rice please?

Ich nehme eine Gemüsesuppe und ein Steak. Aber keine Pommes Frites, bitte. Ich möchte lieber Bratkartoffeln. Geht das? – I will take a vegetable soup and a steak. But no fries, please. I would rather have fried potatoes. Is that possible?

Ja, natürlich! Und was möchten Sie trinken? – Yes, of course! And what would you like to drink?

Eine Cola, bitte – A coke, please.

Und Sie? Was darf ich Ihnen bringen? – And you? What can I bring you?

Einen Hühnchensalat. Und als Vorspeise eine Tomatensuppe, bitte – A chicken salad. And as an appetizer, a tomato soup, please.

Und zu trinken? – And to drink?

Ein Bier, bitte – A beer, please.

Kann ich bitte einen Kuchen bestellen? – Can I please order a cake?

Ich möchte ein Stück Käsekuchen, bitte – I want a piece of the cheesecake, please.

Kommt sofort! – Coming.

Hat es Ihnen geschmeckt? – Was everything good?

Danke, es war ausgezeichnet – Thank you, it was great.

Möchten Sie noch ein Dessert? – Do you want a dessert?

Nein, danke, aber zwei Espresso. Und die Rechnung, bitte – No, thanks, but two espresso. And the bill, please.

Das macht 36 Euro – 36 Euro.

40, bitte. Das stimmt so – 40, please. It is fine.

Danke schön! – Thank you.

Es schmeckt fantastisch/sehr gut/gut. – It tastes fantastic/very good/good.

Nein – No.

Der Salat ist nicht frisch/zu sauer/zu salzig – the salad is not fresh/too sour/too salted.

Die Suppe ist zu scharf/zu salzig – the soup is too hot/salted.

Das Fleisch ist zu kalt/zu fett/zu trocken – the meat is too cold/oily/dry.

Das Brot ist zu trocken/zu alt/zu hart – the bread is too dry/old/too hard.

Das Bier ist zu warm – the beer is too warm.

Entschuldigen Sie, bitte, mit meinem Essen stimmt etwas nicht – Sorry, please, my food is not all right.

Haben Sie bitte frisches Obst? – Do you have fresh fruit, please?

Es sieht schimmelig aus und es riecht komisch – It looks mouldy and it smells weird.

Das Essen ist verdorben – The food is rotten.

Der Steak ist saftig und schmeckt gut. Ich frage mich, wie sie es gemacht haben – The steak is juicy and tastes good. I wonder how they made it.

Die Bananen sind zu reif – The bananas are too ripe.

Die Tomaten sind unreif – The tomatoes are unripe.

Der Reis ist verbrannt – The rice is overdone or overcooked.

Die Kartoffeln sind nicht durch – The potatoes are not done.

Kann ich bitte mit dem Chef sprechen? – Can I please talk to the boss?

Können Sie mir bitte den Rest einpacken? – Can you please pack the rest for me?

Können Sie mir etwas empfehlen? – Can you offer me something?

Some other phrases you could also use are:

Dürfen wir uns an diesen Tisch setzen? – Could we sit at this table, please?

Die Speisekarte, bitte – The menu, please.

Haben Sie eine Speisekarte? – Do you have a menu?

Wir möchten noch ein bisschen überlegen – We want to look a little more.

Können Sie mir bitte Ketchup bringen? – Can you bring me the ketchup please?

Könnte ich noch mehr Soße haben, bitte? – Can I have more sauce, please?

Ich möchte das gleiche – I will have the same.

Können Sie etwas empfehlen? – Is there anything you would recommend?

Haben Sie auch vegetarisches Essen im Angebot? – Do you offer vegetarian food?

Bieten Sie Halal-Gerichte an? – Do you offer halal food?

Ich esse kein Gluten. Gibt es etwas ohne Gluten? – I do not eat gluten. Is there something without gluten?

Ich esse kein Zucker. Können Sie es ohne Zucker zubereiten? – I do not eat sugar. Can you make it without sugar?

Haben Sie koscheres Essen? – Do you have kosher food?

Nein, bitte. Das geht auf mich – No, please. This is on me.

Ich glaube, Sie haben sich verrechnet – I think you have made a mistake.

Also, if you are visiting your friend and they are making a meal for you or you for them, then you could use the following phrases:

Das Essen ist auf dem Tisch. Guten Appetit – The food is on the table. Good appetite.

Lasst es euch schmecken! – Enjoy the meal!

Ich hoffe, dass es euch schmeckt! – I hope that you like it.

Wie hast du das gemacht? – How did you make it?

Es schmeckt fantastisch.Kann ich das Rezept bitte haben? – It tastes fantastic. Could I please have the recipe?

Das Steak ist wunderbar – The steak is wonderful.

Ich habe das Fleisch einfach in ein bisschen Olivenöl, Senf, und Kräutern mariniert. Dann habe ich es in den Ofen gestellt. Ich habe das Rezept aus einem Kochbuch. Ich kann es dir gerne leihen – I just marinated the meat in a bit of olive oil, mustard, and herbs. Then I have put it in the oven. I have the recipe from a cookbook. I can gladly lend it to you.

Ich habe das Rezept aus dem Internet. Du kannst es einfach selbst versuchen – I have the recipe from the Internet. You can try it yourself.

Meine Oma hat ständig diesen Kuchen gebacken als ich klein war. Neulich hat sie mir das Rezept, gegeben und ich bereite es immer wieder zu – My grandma was always baking this cake when I was little. The other day she gave me the recipe, and I keep making it.

Möchtest du Nachschub? – Do you want replenishment?

Möchtest du etwas trinken? – Do you want to drink something?

Möchtest du mehr Wein? – Do you want more wine?

Ich trinke keinen Alkohol – I do not drink alcohol.

Entschuldige bitte, kann ich dir etwas anderes bringen? – Excuse me, can I bring you something else?

Ja, nur Wasser, bitte – Yes, just water, please.

Möchtest du mehr davon haben? – Do you want some more of it?

Kann ich bitte einen Messer für das Steak haben? – Could I please have a knife for the steak?

Könntest du mir bitte eine Serviette geben? – Could you please give me a napkin?

Möchtest du mehr vom Kuchen? – Do you want more cake?

Ja, gerne. Es ist wirklich lecker – Yes, please. It is really delicious.

Wir können gerne mal zusammen kochen – We can cook together sometime.

Das Essen war fantastisch. Vielen Dank – The food was great. Thank you very much.

These were the most important and useful phrases for shopping for groceries and the restaurant.

You may have noticed that when talking about where something is in German, we use words like "vorne" (in the front), "am Eingang" (at the entrance), "neben" (next to) and so on. These words are **PREPOSITIONS**.

Prepositions can have local, temporal, causal, and other meanings. Prepositions stand with the dative, accusative or genitive. So you do not just need to know which preposition is right, but also whether that preposition is followed by a dative, accusative, or genitive.

It is best to learn prepositions in contexts and examples.

A particular challenge for every German learner is the prepositions with local significance. We hope that the following examples, explanations, and exercises help you to use German prepositions correctly.

Are you looking for the right preposition for a particular location? Here you will find the right preposition and the declined article for each location:

Prepositions with local significance – prepositions for places

Local prepositions are:

with dative:

ab, aus, bei, gegenüber von, nach (from, off, by, opposite, after)

Bei dem Fenster – By the window.

Gegenüber vom Tisch – Opposite to the table.

Nach der Ecke – After the corner.

with accusative:

bis, durch, entlang, gegen, um (til, through, along, against, around)

Entlang des Ganges – Along the corridor.

Du fährst um den Supermarkt heru. – You drive around the supermarket.

with dative or accusative (alternating prepositions):

an, auf, hinter, in, neben, über, unter, vor, zwischen (on, on, behind, in, beside, over, under, before, between)

Zwischen dem Tisch und der Küche – Between the table and the kitchen.

Hinter dem Café – Behind the café.

Neben der Ecke – Beside the corner.

When it comes to the dative, we use the following questions:

Wo – Where? => Dative

When it comes to the accusative, we use the following questions:

Wohin? – To where? => Accusative

with genitive:

außerhalb, innerhalb (outside, inside)

Innerhalb des Raumes – Inside the room.

Which preposition do we use with which place?

The preposition depends on the characteristics of the place where we are or where we are going.

An, auf oder in? (on, on or in)

Ich gehe **auf** das Konzert – I am going to the concert.

Ich bin am Meer – I am on the sea.

These prepositions can be followed by a dative (wo?) or accusative (where?).

an = in the immediate vicinity; ganz nah (very close); am Rand (on the edge of something).

am/ans Meer – on/to the sea

Ich gehe ans Meer – I am going to the sea.

am/ans Wasser – on/to the water

Ich bin am Wasser – I am at the water.

am/an den Platz – on/at the place

Ich bin am Platz angekommen – I arrived at the place.

am/an den Strand – on/at the beach

Ich gehe an den Strand – I am going on the beach.

an der/an die Haltestelle – at the/on the bus station

Ich bin an der Haltestelle – I am at the bus station.

am Fenster/ans Fenster – at the window/on the window

Ich habe einen Tisch am Fenster reserviert – I have booked a table at the window.

am Computer/an den Computer – on the computer/to the computer

Ich spiele am Computer – I play on the computer.

auf = a place is open – a place that is higher

auf dem Boden/auf den Boden – on the ground

auf dem/auf den Platz – on the place

auf der/auf die Wiese – on the meadow

auf dem/auf das Feld – on the field

auf dem/auf den Tisch – on the table

auf dem/auf den Berg – on the mountain

auf der/auf die Treppe – on the stairs

in = (closed) rooms; buildings; something around us; mountains; landscapes; places; countries; cardinal points.

im/ins Haus – in the house

Ich bin im Haus – I am in the house.

im/ins Wasser – in the water

Ich springe ins Wasser – I jump in the water.

in der/in die Luft – in the air

Etwas ist in der Luft – Something is in the air.

im/in den Park – in the park

Die Kinder spielen im Park – The children play in the park.

in Berlin – in Berlin

In Berlin gibt es viel zu sehen – In Berlin there is much to see.

in oder nach? (in or after?)

For country names without articles, names of regions without articles, and city names, we use the question "Wohin?" and the preposition "nach".

In Spanien (wo?) – nach Spanien (wohin? – in Spain (where?) – to Spain (to where)

in/an/auf or zu?

The focus is on the way to a place. Whether we really enter the place then remains open in many cases.

Wir gehen in den Supermarkt – We go to the supermarket.

Wir fahren mit dem Auto zum Restaurant – We drive with the car to the restaurant.

We also use the preposition "zu" when we go to a person.

Ich gehe zu Paul – I go to Paul.

Ich bin zum Arzt gegangen – I went to the doctor.

von oder aus?

If we talk about the origin (wo, woher), we use the prepositions von or aus. These two prepositions are always followed by a dative.

Wo? ⇒ in + Dative

Wohin? ⇒ in + Accusative

Woher? ⇒ aus

Wo? ⇒ auf + Dative

Wohin? ⇒ auf + Accusative

Woher? ⇒ von

Wo? ⇒ an + Dative

Wohin? ⇒ an + Accusative

Woher? ⇒ von

Wo? ⇒ bei

Wohin? ⇒ zu

Woher? ⇒ von

The local preposition adverbs draußen, drinnen, oben, unten, rechts, links, vorne, and hinten (out there, inside, up, down, right, left, front, and back) are also important.

Wo? Wohin? Woher?

Draußen, nach draußen/raus, von draußen

Drinnen, nach drinnen/rein, von drinnen

Oben, nach oben/hoch/(he)rauf, von oben

Unten, nach unten/(he)runter, von unten

Vorne, nach vorne/vor, von vorne

Hinten, nach hinten/zurück, von hinten

Hier, hierhin, von hier

Da, dahin, von da

Dort, dorthin, von dort

And another lesson is over!

Chapter 8 – Clothes and Describing Something

Having some knowledge when it comes to clothing and describing materials, your attire, or someone else's style is highly beneficial. Plus, it is another great conversation topic and will be useful when shopping in Germany.

Quick Overview

- Vocabulary
- Phrases for your shopping trip and describing clothing and style
- Demonstrative pronouns
- Indefinite pronouns
- Important verbs
- The passive

Vocabulary

die Kleidung – clothes

die Kopfbedeckungen – headgear

die Mütze – cap

der Hut – hat

die Bademütze – bathing cap

die Badekappe – bathing cap

Schals, T-Shirts, Hemden – scarfs, T-Shirts, shirts

der Schal – scarf

das T-Shirt – T-Shirt

das Hemd – Shirt

die Bluse – blouse

das Polo-Shirt – polo-shirt

der Pullover – sweater

die Jacke – jacket

die Winterjacke – winter jacket

der Mantel – coat

die Hosen – pants

die Jeans – jeans

die Shorts (plural) – shorts

die kurze Hose – shorts

der Rock – skirt

das Kleid – dress

der Anzug – smoking

das Kostüm – costume

Unterwäsche – underwear

die Unterhose – underpants

das Unterhemd – undershirt

die Boxer-Shorts (plural) – boxer shorts

der BH – bra

der Schlafanzug – pajamas

die Socke – sock

die Strumpfhose – tights

der Strumpf – stocking

die Badehose – swimming trunk

der Bikini – bikini

der Badeanzug – swimsuit

die Krawatte – tie

die Fliege – fly

der Gürtel – belt

Schuhe – shoes

der Pantoffel – slipper

die Sandale – sandals

der Sportschuh – sports shoe

der Turnschuh – sneaker

der Lederschuh – leather shoe

der Bergschuh – mountain shoe

der Kletterschuh – climbing shoe

die Badelatsche – flip-flops

die Pumps (plural) – pumps

der Stöckelschuh – stiletto shoe

der Stiefel – boot

der Gummistiefel – rubber boot

der Schmuck – jewelry

Der Schmuck (the jewelery):

das Armband – bracelet

die Ohrringe – earrings

das Halsband – necklace

der Ring – ring

die Taschen – bags

die Handtasche – handbag

die Reisetasche – traveling bag

der Koffer – suitcase

das Täschchen – purse

die Brieftasche – wallet

der Stoff – fabric

die Baumwolle – cotton

die Wolle – wool

(der) Kaschmir – cashmere

das Leder – leather

das Wildleder – suede

das Muster – pattern

Useful adjectives:

geflochten – braided

gestreift – striped

kariert – checkered

gepunktet – dotted

einfach – easy

der Kragen – collar

kragenlos – collarless

der Knopf – button

der V-Ausschnitt – V-neck

das Loch – hole

schön – pretty

hässlich – ugly

modisch/stylisch – stylish

bequem – comfortable

teuer – expensive

billig – cheap

hergestellt in – produced in

lang – long

kurz – short

modern – modern

sportlich – sporty

gross – big

klein – small

einmalig – one of a kind

schick – fashionable

bunt – colorful

aus Baumwolle gemacht – made of cotton

aus Nylon gemacht – made of nylon

neu – new

alt – old

farbig – colored

echt – real

aus Leder – leather

aus Seide – silk

aus Satin – satin

ungewöhnlich – unusual

hell – light

dunkel – dark

dünn – thin

aufreizend – delicate

gebraucht – used

schmal – narrow

weit – wide

eng – tight

locker – loose

bügelfrei – wrinkle resistant

pflegeleicht – easy care

lange Ärmeln – long sleeves

schmutzig – dirty

sauber – clean

You now know the important words when it comes to clothing items. Let's now take a look at the phrases you could use when you shop or talk about clothes.

Let's say that you just arrived in a city and you really need to find the mall. You could ask someone:

Entschuldigen Sie, bitte, wo ist das Einkaufszentrum? – Excuse me, please, where is the mall?

Gibt es ein gutes Einkaufszentrum? – Is there a good mall?

Wo kann man gut shoppen? – Where can I do some shopping?

Wie komme ich zum Einkaufszentrum? – How do I get to the mall?

If you are already in the mall, you may ask for a specific shop:

Entschuldigen Sie, bitte, wo ist C&A? – Excuse me, please, where is C&A?

And if you are looking for a specific piece of cloth, then you will say:

Entschuldigen Sie, bitte, können Sie mir helfen? – Excuse me, please, could you help me?

Ich brauche Hilfe, bitte! – I need help, please.

Ich möchte mir ein T-shirt kaufen – I want to buy myself a T-shirt.

If you want to say that you are looking for something, you can simply say: "Ich suche nach" ("I am looking for"), and after that, you say the name of the item you are looking for.

Ich suche nach Hosen – I am looking for pants.

Ich suche nach blauen Blusen – I am looking for blue blouses.

Ich suche nach grünen Socken – I am looking for green socks.

Or, you can just say that you want to buy something:

Ich möchte einen blauen Rock kaufen – I want to buy a blue skirt.

Ich möchte eine Bluse mit V-Ausschnitt – I want a blouse with a V-neck.

When it comes to sizes, you can simply use the sizes S, M, L, XL, and so on. We use the preposition "in" for the size and the article in the genitive "der". In der Größe S, M, L… – In the size S, M, L…

Haben Sie schwarze Hosen in der Größe XL? – Do you have black pants in the size XL?

Ich brauche dieses T-Shirt in der Größe S – I need this T-shirt in the size S.

Wo finde ich schöne Kleider? – Where can I find nice dresses?

Wo stehen hier die Jacken? – Where are the jackets?

Haben Sie Pullower? – Do you have sweaters?

Kann ich das anprobieren? – Can I try this on?

Ich habe dieses Kleid anprobiert, aber es hat ein Loch. Haben Sie das gleiche Kleid, aber ohne Mängel? – I tried on this dress, but it has a hole. Do you have the same dress, but without this?

Wo sind die Umkleidekabinen? – Where are the changing cabins?

Gibt es das in der Größe M? – Do you have it in size M?

Es ist mir zu klein/groß – It is too small/big.

Die Hosen sind fantastisch, aber sie sind mir zu eng – The pants are great, but they are too tight.

Welche Größe ist das? – Which size is this?

Welche Größe tragen Sie? – What size are you?

Was suchen Sie genau? – What exactly are you looking for?

Wie kann ich Ihnen helfen? – How can I help you?

Möchten Sie es in einer anderen Größe? – Do you want it in another size?

When you want to tell someone how you feel about the item, you can say the following:

Mir gefällt die Farbe/der Stoff sehr gut – I like the color/fabric.

Das Modell ist schön, aber ich trage sowas nicht – The model is nice, but I do not wear this.

Ich mag es nicht – I do not like it.

Ich mag den Ausschnitt nicht – I do not like the clipping.

Es passt/Es passt nicht – It fits/It does not fit.

Es passt sehr gut zu Ihrer Figur. Sie sehen schlank darin aus – It fits great to your figure. You look slim in it.

Ich nehme es – I will take it.

Ich schaue mich noch etwas um – I will look around a bit more.

Können Sie mir es bitte einpacken? – Can you please pack it for me?

Wieviel kostet das? – How much is this?

Das ist mir zu teuer – This is too expensive for me.

Wie möchten Sie zahlen? – How do you want to pay?

Mit Bargeld oder Kreditkarte? – Cash or credit card?

Kreditkarte, bitte – Credit card, please.

Kann ich mit Kreditkarte zahlen? – Can I pay with credit card?

Wann schließen Sie? – When are you closing?

Wann öffnen Sie? – When are you opening?

Bis wann haben Sie offen? – Until when are you open?

Das macht 23 Euro – This makes 23 Euro.

Geben Sie bitte den Code ein – Type the code please.

Die Kreditkarte wurde abgelehnt – The card was rejected.

Können Sie es bitte erneut versuchen? – Can you please try it one more time?

Vielen Dank für Ihre Hilfe – Thank you very much for the help.

Kommen Sie bald wieder – Come again soon.

Gibt es ein Restaurant im Einkaufszentrum? – Is there a restaurant in the mall?

Wo ist die Toilette? – Where is the toilet?

Haben Sie irgendwo noch eine weitere Filiale? – Do you have another subsidiary somewhere else?

If you are talking to a friend about clothes or if you shop together, these phrases could help you a lot:

Ich liebe schwarze Klamotten – I love black clothes.

Mir gefällt dein neuer Pullower! – I like your new sweater.

Ich muss ein Geschenk kaufen – I need to buy a present.

Das T-Shirt ist sehr schön und modern – The T-shirt is very beautiful and modern.

Es hat Flecken – It has spots.

Es hat Knöpfe – It has buttons.

Ich finde du siehst toll in dem Kleid aus – I think you look amazing in that dress.

Diese Jeans sehen zu eng aus – The jeans look too tight.

Du siehst darin schlank aus – You look slim in it.

Es steht dir sehr gut – It fits very well on you.

Es sieht nicht gut aus – It looks bad.

Mir gefällt die Farbe nicht – I do not like the color.

Du solltest etwas anderes anprobieren – You should try something else.

Wie sehe ich aus? – How do I look?

Steht mir das? – Does this fit good?

Ich fühle mich nicht wohl darin – I do not feel well in it.

Was denkst du über diesen Pullower, diese Bluse, dieses Hemd? – What do you think about this sweater, blouse, shirt?

Dieses Hemd möchte ich für meinen Freund kaufen – I want to buy this shirt for my boyfriend.

Meine Freundin trägt gerne farbige Hosen – My girlfriend likes to wear colorful pants.

Ich habe eine schöne Jacke im Laden gesehen – I saw a nice jacket in the shop.

Sie ist weiß, sportlich, locker, und aus Nylon gemacht – It is white, sporty, loose, and made of nylon.

Es kostet nur 20 Euro – It is just 20 Euro.

Ich habe sehr viele alte Mützen – I have many old caps.

Meine Schwester trägt bunte Kleidung – My sister wears colorful clothes.

Mein Bruder trägt nur schwarz – My brother only wears black.

Wo hast du diesen Rock gekauft? – Where have you bought this skirt?

Wann hast du diese Jeans gekauft? – When did you buy these jeans?

Der Schal sieht cool aus – The scarf looks cool.

Ich mag deinen Stil – I like your style.

Möchtest du mit mir einkaufen gehen? – Do you want to go shopping with me?

Lass uns einkaufen gehen! – Let's go shopping!

We will now go over some grammar. You may have noticed the words "diese, diesen..."

For example: Wo hast du diesen Rock gekauft?

What type of words are they? Pronouns. Only this time, they are **DEMONSTRATIVE PRONOUNS** as they refer to people or things nearby. They are declined like certain articles:

N masculine

dieser Rock

G

dieses Rockes

D

diesem Rock

A

diesen Rock

N feminine

diese Tasche

G

dieser Tasche

D

dieser Tasche

A

diese Tasche

N neutral

dieses Kleid

G

dieses Kleides

D

diesem Kleid

A

dieses Kleid

N Plural

diese Schuhe

G

dieser Schuhe

D

diesen Schuhen

A

diese Schuhe

Examples:

Magst du diese Schuhe? – Do you like those shoes?

Ich möchte diesen Rock kaufen – I want to buy this rock.

Du kannst es mit dieser Bluse kombinieren – You can combine it with this blouse.

Now is also the perfect time for you to learn about another type of pronoun: **INDEFINITE PRONOUNS**.

The indefinite pronouns stand for an unspecified or more precisely designated person or thing. They are used substantively or adjectively.

The indefinite pronouns include:

Einer (one)

Keiner (none)

Irgendein (any)

Irgendwer (anyone)

Jeder (anyone)

Jedermann (everyone)

jeglicher (anyone)

jemand (someone)

niemand (noone)

kein(er)(no)

alles (everything)

nichts (nothing)

man (one)

einige (come)

etliche (some)

etwas (something)

sämtliche (all)

While "man", "etwas", and "nichts" remain unchanged, declined they are:

jemand – niemand – jedermann – jemand anderer

Nominative, jemand, niemand

Genitive, jemandes, niemandes

Dative, jemand(em), niemand(em)

Accusative, jemand(en), niemand(en)

Dieses Hemd gehört niemandem – This shirt belongs to nobody.

Die Hosen kann man bügeln – The pants can be ironed.

Das ist jemandes Auto – This is someone's car.

It is also useful to get to know the preposition "von" (from/of). "Von" can be used with names. You can say:

Das ist Marias Bluse – This is Maria's blouse.

Or

Das ist die Bluse **von** Maria – This is the blouse of Maria.

"Von" with a name means possession or the origin of things or people.

Niklas ist der Vater von Maria – Niklas is the father of Maria.

Let's now go over the **important verbs** from the lesson:

Most verbs from the lesson are conjugated regularly. We want to focus on the verbs:

stehen

gefallen

passen

Many German verbs require an object. Often it is an object in the accusative. Some German verbs need an object in the dative. The dative object often indicates the target or recipient of an action and is therefore often a person. The verbs we listed belong to this group.

Das T-Shirt passt dem Mann nicht – The T-shirt does not fit the man.

Die Bluse steht der Frau – The blouse looks nice on the woman.

Die Jacke gefällt dem Mädchen – The girl likes the jacket.

You can also use a personal pronoun as a dative object. To do this, you have to put the personal pronoun in the dative:

Ich – mir

Du – dir

<u>Examples:</u>

Das Hemd passt mir nicht – The shirt does not suit me.

Der Pullover steht dir nicht – The sweater does not fit you.

The verbs with a dative object can be set to **PASSIVE**.

The passive is used when the most important information in the sentence is an activity and not the performer.

Das Kleid wird gekauft – The dress is bought.

The passive is formed with the conjugated auxiliary verb "werden" and the participle II (it was explained in one of the previous lessons) at the end of the sentence.

Active

Ich koche das Abendessen – I cook the dinner.

Der Lehrer korrigiert die Tests – The teacher is correcting the tests.

Passive

Das Abendessen wird gekocht – The dinner is being cooked.

Die Tests werden korrigiert – The tests are being corrected.

The performer can be expressed as "von + Dativ".

Das Abendessen wird von mir gekocht – The dinner is being cooked by me.

Die Tests werden vom Lehrer korrigiert – The tests are being corrected by the teacher.

Passive preterite

The passive preterite is formed with the preterite form of "werden" and the participle II of the verb.

Ich werde in einer Schule ausgebildet – I am being trained in a school.

Ich wurde in einer Schule ausgebildet – I was trained in a school.

And that concludes this lesson!

Chapter 9 – Accommodation and Transport

Wherever you go, accommodation and transport are very important. You will probably need to catch a cab to a hotel, or maybe you will need to get around by car. When you arrive at your accommodation, you will also need some phrases to book a room or report an issue. Thus, you need to know basic phrases and sentences. However, of course, just like any other lesson, you first need to know the vocabulary.

Quick Overview

- Vocabulary
- Phrases for describing the way—for transport and accommodation
- Important verbs
- Subjunctive II
- Future I

Vocabulary

der Verkehr – traffic

die Ampel – traffic lights

der Reflektor – reflector

der Umweg – detour

die Umleitung – diversion

die Abkürzung – abbreviation

der Unfall – accident

die Markierung – mark

der Strich – line

das Verkehrsschild – sign

die Bundesstraße – federal highway

die Autobahn – highway

der Weg – way

das Tempolimit – speed limit

der Blitzer – speed camera

bremsen – slow down

beschleunigen – accelerate

der Fußgängerüberweg – pedestrian crossing

die Unterführung – underpass

die Brücke – bridge

der Zebrastreifen – crosswalk

der Bürgersteig – sidewalk

der Verkehrsstau – traffic jam

der Anhänger – trailer

die Straßenbauarbeiten – road works

der Nahverkehr – local traffic

der Individualverkehr – individual traffic

das Autobahnkreuz – motorway junction

die Einfahrt – entrance

die Ausfahrt – exit

die Einmündung – junction

die Abzweigung – turn off

die Verkehrsmittel – transport

das Auto – car

das Flugzeug – plane

der Zug – train

der Bus – bus

das Fahrrad – bicycle

zu Fuß – by foot

die Spur – track

die Tankstelle – gas station

die Raststätte – service area

der Parkplatz – parking lot

der Müll – garbage

die Schiene – rail

der Fahrplan – timetable

der Stadtplan – city map

die Bäckerei – bakery

das Ticket – ticket

der Automat – machine

die Anzeigetafel – scoreboard

die Rolltreppe – escalator

der Lift – lift, elevator

das Gepäck – luggage

rechts/links – right/left

der Aufenthalt – stay

die Aufgabe, die Aufgaben – task, duty

der Ausweis – ID card

die Badewanne – bathtub

das Einzelzimmer – single room

das Doppelzimmer – double room

das Frühstücksbüffet – breakfast buffet

der Gang – hallway

das Haustier – pet

der Hotelmanager – hotel manager (male)

die Hotelmanagerin – hotel manager (female)

inbegriffen – included

die Pension – guesthouse

der Reisepass – passport

die Rezeption – reception

der Rezeptionist – receptionist (male)

die Rezeptionistin – receptionist (female)

der Roomboy – housekeeping (male)

das Zimmermädchen – housekeeping (female)

das Badezimmer – bathroom

der Dach – roof

die Decke – ceiling

das Fenster – window

der Fußboden – floor

der Balkon – balcony

die Küche – kitchen

das Schlafzimmer – bedroom

die Toilette – toilet

die Treppe – stairs

die Tür – door

die Wand – wall

das Wohnzimmer – living room

das Badezimmer – bathroom

der Keller – basement

das Esszimmer – dining room

das Stockwerk – floor

die Garage – garage

das Erdgeschoss – ground floor

das Gästezimmer – guest room

der Dachboden – loft

die Möbel – furniture

der Schrank – cupboard

das Sofa – sofa

der Sessel – armchair

das Bett – bed

der Tisch – table

der Kleiderschrank – wardrobe

der Stuhl – chair

der Schreibtisch – desk

die Dusche – shower

das Regal – shelf

die Waschmaschine – washing machine

der Kühlschrank – refrigerator

die Spülmaschine – dishwasher

der Teppich – carpet

die Lampe – lamp

der Fernseher – TV

die Sauna – sauna

der Schlafsaal – dormitory

die Übernachtung – overnight stay

das Büfett – buffet

das Hotel – hotel

das Luxushotel – luxury hotel

die Lobby – lobby

die Hotelbar – hotel bar

das Hotelrestaurant – restaurant

der Wellnessbereich – spa

der Pool – pool

der Portier – doorman

der Kofferträger – bellboy

der Concierge – concierge

der Koch – cook

der Kellner – waiter

der Butler – butler

das Trinkgeld – tip

die Reservierung – reservation

die Buchung – booking

der Check-In – check-in

der Check-Out – check-out

der Service – service

der Zimmerschlüssel – room key

die Schlüsselkarte – keycard

das Einzelbett – single bed

das Doppelbett – double bed

die getrennten Betten – separated beds (in a TWIN room)

der Kleiderschrank – dresser

der Nachttisch – nightstand

die Nachttischlampe – bedside lamp

die Heizung – heater

die Klimaanlage – air conditioner

das Zimmer mit Meerblick – room with seaview

So, you got the vocabulary? Let's see what you will need when you arrive in the city.

Here are the most important phrases for your trip and stay regarding accommodation:

Entschuldigen Sie bitte, wie komme ich zum Stadtzentrum? – Excuse me, how do I get to the city center?

Wo kann ich parken? – Where can I park?

Wo befindet sich die Bushaltestelle? – Where is the bus station?

Wo befindet sich das Hotel? – Where is the hotel?

Wie komme ich zum Flughafen? – How do I get to the airport?

Ich suche den Marienplatz. Können Sie mir bitte helfen? – I am looking for the Marienplatz. Could you please help me?

Wo befindet sich die Kirche? – Where is the church?

Ich suche eine Post. Wo kann ich eine finden? – I am looking for a post office. Where can I find one?

Being able to describe the way is very important so that you can almost always find your way abroad when someone tells you the way. In addition, you may also be able to help tourists who ask you for directions. So memorize the phrases carefully and remember the important terms!

Sie gehen einfach die Straße entlang und biegen dann rechts an der Ecke ab. Dann fahren Sie noch ein paar Meter geradeaus und dort werden Sie ihr Hotel sehen – You just walk down the street and then turn right at the corner. Then go straight for a few more meters and there you will see your hotel.

Remember the following terms:

links – left

rechts – right

geradeaus – straight on

entlang gehen – to go along

hinunter gehen – to go down

gehe (...) für (...) Meter entlang – follow (...) for (...) meters

bis du (das) (...) erreichst – until you reach (the) (...)

rechts/links abbiegen – to turn right/left

vorbeigehen – to go past

über die Brücke gehen – to go over the bridge

etwas überqueren – to cross something

Another example:

First, walk down Kirchstraße until you reach the hospital. There you turn right into the Jahnstraße. Pass the museum and the cinema and cross the Bachstraße. Go over the bridge and then turn left. Just follow the Poststraße for about 200 meters and then you can see the hotel on the right.

Zuerst gehen Sie die Kirchstraße entlang, bis Sie das Krankenhaus erreichen. Dort biegen Sie rechts in die Jahnstraße ab. Gehen Sie an dem Museum und dem Kino vorbei und überqueren Sie die Bachstraße. Gehen Sie über die Brücke und dann biegen Sie links ab. Folgen Sie einfach der Poststraße für etwa 200 Meter und dann können Sie das Hotel auf der rechten Seite sehen.

If you need to ask someone when the bus or train arrives, you simply ask:

Entschuldigen Sie bitte, wann kommt der nächste Zug für...? – Excuse me, when does the next train to... arrive?

Wo kann ich ein Ticket für den Bus kaufen? – Where can I buy a ticket for the bus?

Wie viel kostet ein Ticket? – How much does the ticket cost?

Wo kann ich den Fahrplan sehen? – Where can I see the timetable?

Wo kann ich ein Zimmer mieten? – Where can I rent a room?

Ich suche nach einem Hostel in der Nähe des Stadtzentrums. Wissen Sie vielleicht, wo es eins gibt? – I am looking for a hostel near the city center. Do you know where there is one?

Ich habe ein Zimmer in dem ___ hotel gebucht. Wo befindet sich dieses Hotel? Wie komme ich zum Hotel? – I booked a room in the ___ hotel. Where is this hotel located? How do I get to the hotel?

Gibt es in der Stadt eine Frühstückspension? – Is there a bed and breakfast in the city?

Ich bin als Backpacker unterwegs. Wo kann ich einen Campingplatz finden? Wie komme ich zum ersten Campingplatz? Wie lange werde ich zu Fuß brauchen? – I am traveling as a backpacker. Where can I find a campsite? How do I get to the first campsite? How long will I need to walk?

Ich möchte gerne ein Zimmer reservieren – I would like to book a room.

Ich brauche ein Zimmer – I need a room.

Was für ein Zimmer möchten Sie? – What type of room do you want?

Ich möchte ein Doppelzimmer, bitte – I want a double room, please.

Ich möchte ein Zimmer mit schönem Ausblick – I want a room with a nice view.

Wieviel kostet eine Nacht? – How much does one night cost?

Ich kenne mich nicht sehr gut aus. Ich suche nach einer Unterkunft. Wie sind die Preise hier so? – I do not know this place very well. I am looking for a place to stay. How are the prices here?

Ich brauche dringend ein Zimmer. Sind noch irgendwelche Zimmer frei? – I need a room urgently. Are any rooms available?

Gibt es etwas billigeres? – Is there anything cheaper?

Ich möchte ein Zimmer für drei Nächte mit Frühstück inklusive buchen – I want to book a room for three nights with breakfast included.

Können Sie mir mein Zimmer zeigen? – Can you show me my room?

Wieviel kostet ein Zimmer für ___ Personen? – How much is a room for ___ people? I would like to book ___ .

Ich möchte eine Unterkunft für ____ Personen buchen. Was empfehlen Sie mir? – I would like to book accommodation for ____ people. What do you recommend?

Was ist im Preis erhalten? Ist Frühstück inklusive? – What is included in the price? Is breakfast included?

Gibt es Handtücher und Bettwäsche in der Unterkunft? – Are there towels and sheets in the accommodation?

Sind Tiere erlaubt? – Are pets allowed?

Ich bringe meinen Hund mit. Gibt es ein Tierhotel? – I am bringing my dog. Is there a pet hotel?

Verfügen Sie über eine Garage/einen Parkplatz? Ist das inklusive? – Do you have a garage/parking space? Is it inclusive?

Ich brauche einen Safe. Haben Sie einen? – I need a safe. Do you have one?

Können Sie mir den Schlüssel für das Zimmer Nummer ___ geben? – Can you give me the key for room number ___?

Haben Sie ein Telefon? Ich muss telefonieren – Do you have a telephone? I have to make a call.

Um wieviel Uhr wird das Frühstück serviert? – At what time is breakfast being served?

Ich muss morgen um ___ Uhr aufstehen. Können Sie mich bitte aufwecken? – I have to get up tomorrow at ___ o'clock. Can you wake me up please?

Ich brauche ein Taxi zum Stadtzentrum. Könnten Sie bitte eins rufen? – I need a taxi to the city center. Could you please call one?

Kann ich das Internet hier utzen? Wie lautet das Password? – Can I use the Internet here? What is the password?

Ich bin zum ersten Mal in der Stadt. Was gibt es in der Nähe so alles? Was sollte ich mir hier ansehen? – This is my first time in the city. Is there anything here nearby? What should I go see?

Ich gehe jetzt die Stadt besichtigen. Könnten Sie bitte in der Zwischenzeit mein Zimmer reinigen? – I am going to visit the city now. Could you please clean my room in the meantime?

Ich möchte nicht, dass das Zimmer jetzt gereinigt wird. Können Sie später/morgen kommen? – I do not want the room to be cleaned now. Can you come later/tomorrow?

Das Zimmer ist jetzt besetzt – The room is occupied.

Entschuldigung, könnte ich meinen Schlüssel bekommen? – Excuse me, could I get my keys?

Wo ist der Empfang? – Where is the reception?

Wann ist Frühstück/Mittagessen/Abendessen? – At what time is breakfast/lunch/dinner?

Könnte ich bitte Zimmerservice bestellen? – Can I please order room service?

Bis wann muss ich auschecken? – When do I have to check out?

Haben Sie bitte noch ein Handtuch/Bettlaken? – Do you have another towel/bed sheet?

Könnte ich bitte die Rechnung bekommen? – Can I please have the bill?

Mein Zimmer gefällt mir nicht – I do not like my room.

Kann ich bitte ein anderes bekommen? – Could I please get another one?

Entschuldigen Sie, bitte. Meine Nachbarn sind zu laut. Ich kann nicht schlafen. Könnten Sie etwas dagegen machen? – Excuse me, please. My neighbors are too loud. I cannot sleep. Can you do something about it?

Ich möchte ein anderes Zimmer. Es ist schmutzig/zu kalt/zu warm/unordentlich – I want another room. It is dirty/too cold/too hot/untidy.

In meinem Zimmer riecht es komisch. Kann ich bitte ein anderes Zimmer bekommen? – It smells weird in my room. Can I get another room please?

Können Sie mir bitte helfen? In meinem Zimmer gibt es kein warmes Wasser – Could you please help me? There is no warm water in my room.

Ich bin unzufrieden mit meinem Zimmer/Ihrem Service. Ich möchte gerne auschecken – I am dissatisfied with my room/service. I would like to check-out.

Mir gefällt es hier nicht. Können Sie mir ein anderes Hotel empfehlen? – I do not like it here. Could you recommend another hotel?

Ich würde gerne mit Kreditkarte zahlen – I would like to pay with my credit card.

Ich hätte gerne ein anderes Zimmer – I would like another room.

Würden Sie mir bitte das Frühstück ins Zimmer bringen? – Could you bring me the breakfast in my room?

Ich brauche dringend einen Platz zum Übernachten. Hätten Sie noch ein Zimmer frei? – I urgently need a place to stay. Would you have another free room?

Ich habe morgen ein Meeting mit einigen Geschäftspartnern. Wo könnte man in der Nähe schön essen? Es sollte ruhiger sein – I have a meeting tomorrow with some business partners. Where can one eat something nice in the area? It should be quieter.

Haben Sie ein Fitnessbereich? Ich möchte gerne trainieren – Do you have a gym? I would like to train.

Kann ich einen Fitnesstrainer buchen? – Can I get a personal trainer?

Ich brauche ein Fitnessstudio für 7 Tage. Wieviel würde das kosten? – I need a gym for 7 days. How much would it cost?

Wo ist der Pool? – Where is the pool?

Ich würde gerne die Sauna benutzen – I would like to use the sauna.

Wie komme ich zum Einkaufszentrum? – How do I get to the mall?

Könnte ich mit der U-Bahn zum Stadtzentrum kommen? – Could I catch the subway to the city center?

Mir gefällt es hier wirklich gut. Ich würde das Zimmer gerne für eine weitere Nacht buchen – I really like it here. I would like to book the room for one more night.

Alles war fantastisch. Vielen Dank! Wir werden sicher wieder kommen – Everything was fantastic. Thank you very much! We will come again for sure.

If you need to rent an apartment at some point, here are some phrases you might need.

When you want to book an appointment to see the apartment:

Könnte ich mit dem Apartmentmanager sprechen? – Could I talk to the apartment manager?

Ja, natürlich. Das bin ich – Yes, of course. That is me.

Ich rufe Sie wegen des Apartments in der Bachstraße an – I am calling you because of the apartment in the Bachstraße.

Alles klar. Möchten Sie es sich ansehen? – All right. Do you want to take a look at it?

Ja, ich würde es liebend gern sehen – Yes, I would really love to see it.

Passt Freitag um 17 Uhr? – Is Friday at 5 o'clock good?

Ja, das passt sehr gut – Yes, that fits good.

Wissen Sie, wie Sie hierher kommen können? – Do you know how to get here?

Ja, ich werde mich zurechtfinden – Yes, I will find the way.

Muss ich irgendetwas mitbringen? – Do I need to bring anything?

Nein, Sie müssen nur sich selbst mitbringen – No, you just need to come and be there.

Ist das Apartment frei. Ich bin daran interessiert und würde es mir gerne ansehen – Is the apartment free? I am interested and would like to see it.

Kann ich heute Nachmittag kommen? – Can I come today in the afternoon?

Ja, kommen Sie doch um 16 Uhr – Yes, you can come at 4 o'clock.

Super. Wir sehen uns um 16 Uhr. Kennen Sie die Adresse? – Great. We will see each other at 4. Do you know where it is?

Ja, ich kenne mich in dieser Gegend gut aus – Yes, I get around this area very well.

Und bitte bringen Sie Ihren Ausweis mit – And please bring your ID card.

Können Sie mir etwas mehr Informationen über Ihre Wohnung geben? – Can you give me a little more information about your apartment?

Ich brauche einige Informationen – I need some information.

Natürlich. Wie kann ich Ihnen helfen? – Sure, what can I help you with?

Ich möchte gerne wissen, welche Art von Transportmittel es in der Nähe des Apartments gibt. Wie komme ich z.B. zum Stadtzentrum? – I would like to know what type of transport is available near the apartment. How do I get to the city center for instance?

Ich bin mir nicht wirklich sicher, aber ich denke, dass es einen Bahnhof in der Nähe gibt. Ich kann für Sie nachsehen, wenn Sie wollen? – I am not really sure, but I think that there is a train station nearby. I can look it up for you if you want?

*Wissen Sie, in welche Richtung der Zug fährt und gibt es einen Fahrplan? – Do you know what direction that train goes and is there a timetable?

Es tut mir leid, aber das weiß ich nicht. Ich kann im Internet nachsehen. Sie können aber auch selbst nachsehen, wenn Sie mehr Informationen brauchen – I am sorry, but I do not know that. I can check the Internet. You can also look for yourself if you need more information.

Alles klar. Macht nichts. Ich sehe es mir selbst an. Vielen Dank für die Hilfe – All right. Never mind. I will take a look at it. Many thanks for the help.

Viel Glück bei der Suche – Good luck with your search.

If you are searching for a roommate, you could use the following phrases:

Hallo, spreche ich mit Marcus? – Hi, am I speaking with Marcus?

Ja, der bin ich. Mit wem spreche ich? – Yes, I am he. With whom am I speaking?

Oh, entschuldige, bitte. Thomas am Apparat. Du hast mir eine E-Mail für das Apartment geschrieben. Ich bin auf der Suche nach einem Mitbewohner – Oh, sorry, Thomas on the phone. You wrote me an email for the apartment. I am looking for a roommate.

Ach so. Ja, das habe ich – Ah, yes, I did.

Also, ich wollte mal anrufen und ein wenig mit dir sprechen, bevor wir uns treffen. Ich brauche einige Informationen – Well, I wanted to call and talk to you a little before we meet. I need some information.

Alles klar. Du kannst ruhig fragen – All right. You are free to ask me.

Ich denke, dass wir schon gut miteiander auskommen müssen, damit alles klappt. Deswegen wollte ich dich fragen, wie du so bist und ob es irgendwas gibt, was ich wissen sollte – I think that we have to get along well together so that everything works out. That is why I wanted to ask you how you are and if there is anything I should know.

Ja, ich verstehe. Ich bin derselben Meinung. Also, ich bin ein ganz normaler Typ. Ich konzentriere mich auf mein Studium und ich lerne jeden Tag sehr viel. Ich bin eher ein ruhiger Typ und ich kann mich gut mit fast jedem verstehen. Ich bin ein einfacher Mensch – Yes, I understand. I got the same opinion. Well, I am a normal guy. I concentrate on my studies and I learn a lot every day. I am more of a quiet guy and I am good with almost anyone. I am a simple person.

Super. Mir gefällt das. Ich bin auch sehr bodenständig und ruhig. Rauchst du? Trinkst du Alkohol? – Super. I like that. I am also very down to earth and calm. Do you smoke? Do you drink alcohol?

Nein, ich habe vor drei Jahren mit dem Rauchen aufgehört, und wenn es um Alkohol geht, trinke ich manchmal am Wochenende, aber das ist nicht sehr oft – No, I quit smoking three years ago, and when it comes to alcohol, I sometimes drink on weekends, but it is not very often.

Alles klar. Das ist in Ordnung. Hast du irgendwelche Fragen an mich? – All right. That is fine. Do you have any questions for me?

Ja, schon. Gibt es einen Parkplatz vor dem Gebäude? – Yes, actually. Is there a parking lot in front of the building?

Nein. Leider musst du in der Straße parken. Aber es ist sicher – No. Unfortunately, you have to park in the street. But it is safe.

Ja, das ist schade. Aber damit kann ich leben. Ich würde trotzdem gerne einziehen – Yes, this is a pity. But I can live with it. I would like to move in anyway.

Das sind großartige Neuigkeiten! Wann möchtest du kommen und einziehen? – Great news! When would you like to come and move in?

Ist Montag in Ordnung? Da werde ich auch meine Sachen mitbringen können – Is Monday all right? I will also be able to bring my things with me.

Kein Problem. Das passt. Ich werde da sein – No problem. That fits. I will be there.

If you need to ask some more questions, like something about the neighborhood, then the following phrases will help you:

Hallo, ich muss nach ein paar mehr Informationen fragen – Hi, I need to ask for some more information.

Ja, gerne. Was interessiert Sie? – Yes, gladly. What interests you?

Mich interessiert die Nachbarschaft in der Gegend in der sich das Apartment befindet – I am interested in the neighborhood in the area where the apartment is located.

Natürlich. Was genau möchten Sie wissen? – What would you like to know?

Was können Sie mir darüber sagen? Wie sind die Nachbarn? Wie ist die Gegend allgemein? – What can you tell me about it? How are the neighbors? How is the neighborhood in general?

Um ehrlich zu sein, die Nachbarn sind wunderbar. Sehr nett und freundlich. Aber die Gegend ist schon nicht die beste – To be honest, the neighbors are wonderful. Very nice and friendly. But the area is not the best.

Wie meinen Sie das? – What do you mean by that?

Na ja, die Straßen sind manchmal schmutzig, und niemand kümmert sichwirklich darum. Es ist nicht schrecklich, aber es ist auch nicht schön. Außer dem Müll gibt es aber keine anderen Beschwerden – Well, the streets are dirty sometimes, and no one really cares. It is not terrible, but it is not pretty. Apart from the garbage, there are no other complaints.

Gab es jemals Probleme mit den Nachbarn? Muss ich auf irgendetwas aufpassen? – Have you ever had problems with the neighbors? Do I have to take care of anything?

Nein, eigentlich nicht. Alle sind freundlich, wie gesagt, und niemand wird Sie stören – No, not really. Everyone is friendly, as I said, and nobody will disturb you.

Gut. Ich hoffe aber, dass das Problem mit dem Müll gelöst wird. Das ist wirklich sehr schade – All right. But I hope that the problem with the garbage will be solved. That is a pity.

Ich teile Ihre Meinung, und hoffe auch, dass es besser wird – I share your opinion, and I hope it will get better.

When you finally decide you want the apartment, it is time to negotiate the price:

Ich habe mich entschieden. Ich möchte dieses Apartment mieten – I have decided. I want to rent this apartment.

Das freut mich sehr – I am really happy about that.

Wieviel würde ein Monat kosten? – How much would a month be?

Ich vermiete dieses Apartment für 900 Euro pro Monat – I rent this apartment for 900 Euro per month.

Das ist aber sehr viel für nur einen Monat – This is pretty much just for one month.

Das ist ein fairer Preis – That us a fair price.

Was sagen Sie zu 750 Euro pro Monat? – What do you say about 750 Euro per month?

Das passt mir leider nicht – That does not fit me.

Ich lasse mich auf 800 Euro ein oder gar nicht – I can give 800 Euro or nothing.

Unter 900 gehe ich nicht – I am not going under 900.

Können Sie bitte mit dem Preis etwas runter gehen? – Could you please go lower?

Nein, leider nicht – No, unfortunately not.

If you have pets and want to ask about the policy regarding animals, then you could use the following:

Sind Tiere im Gebäude erlaubt? – Are pets allowed in the building?

Haustiere sind schon erlaubt, aber Sie müssen zusätzliche zweihundert Euro Kaution hinterlegen – We do allow pets, but you must pay an additional two hundred Euro security deposit.

Sind alle Tiere erlaubt? – Are all animals allowed?

Leider nein. Sie können nur einen Hund oder eine Katze haben – Unfortunately not. You can just have one cat or one dog.

Alles klar. Gibt es in der Nähe einen Park oder Straße, wo ich mit meinem Haustier spazieren gehen kann? – All right. Is there a park or street nearby where I can go for a walk with my pet?

Ja, es gibt einen schönen Park für Tiere gleich um die Ecke – Yes, there is a nice park for animals just around the corner.

Gibt es im Gebäude noch andere Bewohner, die ein Haustier haben? – Are there any residents in the building who have pets?

Nicht viele, aber es gibt ein paar mit denen Sie zusammen mit den Haustieren spazieren gehen können – Not many, but there are a few that you can go for a walk with your pets.

If you need to talk to a moving company so that they can help you move in, then you can use the following:

Hallo, wie geht es Ihnen? – Hello, how are you doing?

Gut danke. Ich könnte etwas Hilfe beim Umzug in eine neue Wohnung gebrauchen – Good, thank you. I could use some help in moving to a new apartment.

Alles klar, wie können wir helfen? – All right, how can we help?

Ich muss einige Möbel von meiner alten in die neue Wohnung transportieren – I have to transport some furniture from my old to the new apartment.

In Ordnung. Kein Problem. Geben Sie mir bitte die Adressen von beiden Wohnungen, und wir machen den Rest für Sie – All right. No problem. Please give me the addresses of both apartments, and we will do the rest for you.

Super, danke – Great, thanks.

Könnten Sie mir nur sagen, welcher Tag für Sie am besten passt und um welche Zeit Sie möchten, dass wir die Arbeit erledigen? – Could you just tell me what day works for you best and around what time you would like us to do the job?

Passt Dienstag um 12 Uhr? – Is Tuesday at 12 o'clock good?

Ja, das passt – Yes, that is fine.

If you need to speak to the neighbor, then you can use these phrases:

Hallo, ich bin der neue Nachbar. Ich könnte ein paar Informationen gebrauchen – Hello, I am the new neighbor. I could use some information.

Natürlich, was interessiert Sie? – Of course, what interests you?

Ich habe bemerkt, dass hier alle sehr freundlich sind. Sie kennen sich hier alle gut oder? – I noticed that everyone here is very friendly. Does everyone know each other well here?

Ja, die meisten von uns leben hier schon seit mehr als zehn Jahren. Deswegen sind wir so entspannt und freundlich zueinander – Yes, most of us have lived here for more than ten years. That is why we are so relaxed and friendly to each other.

Ach so, wie lange leben Sie schon hier? – Oh okay, how long have you been living here?

Ich glaube es sind schon 12 Jahre – I think it has already been 12 years.

Dann wäre es super, wenn Sie mir sagen könnten, was sich so alles in der Gegend befindet und wo ich Lebensmittel einkaufen kann – It would be great if you could tell me what is in the area and where I can buy groceries.

Natürlich. Ich kenne mich sehr gut aus. Wenn Sie wollen, können Sie mit mir morgen in den Supermarkt gehen. So werden Sie sich den Weg merken – Of course. I know this block well. If you want, you can go to the supermarket with me tomorrow. So you will remember the way.

Das wäre super – That would be great.

Gut, dann lassen Sie uns morgen um 10 Uhr losfahren. Passt das? – Good, then we can go tomorrow at 10 o'clock. Does it fit?

Ja, klar. Vielen Dank – Yes, sure. Thank you very much.

When you need to ask if there can be visitors or extra people in the apartment, you can use the following:

Ich habe eine Frage. Dürfen zusätzliche Leute in meiner Wohnung leben? – I have a question. May additional people live in my apartment?

Sie können einen Mitbewohner haben, aber Sie müssen erst unsere Genehmigung dafür bekommen. Sie müssen auch ein Formular ausfüllen und unterschreiben – You can have a roommate, but you must first get our permission. You also have to fill in and sign a form.

Und kann jemand zum Übernachten kommen? – And can someone come to sleep over?

Ja, wenn jemand ab und zu kommt, um zu übernachten, dann ist das in Ordnung – Yes, if somebody comes every now and then to stay overnight, that is fine.

Wieviele Tage darf dieser Gast denn bleiben? – How many days is this guest allowed to stay?

Eine Woche maximal. Wenn der Gast länger bleibt, dann müssen wir nachprüfen, ob es sich wirklich nur um einen Gast handelt – If the guest stays longer, then we have to check if it really is just a guest.

Muss ich für extra Gäste und Besucher bezahlen? – Do I have to pay for extra guests and visitors?

Wenn wir die Besucher erlauben und diese länger bleiben wollen, dann müssen Sie wahrscheinlich bezahlen – If we allow the visitors and they want to stay longer, then you will probably have to pay.

Können meine Gäste die Wäscherei benutzen? – Can my guests use the laundry?

Das können Ihre Gäste machen, aber Sie müssen den Gast dabei begleiten – Your guests can do that, but you have to be there with the guest.

If you, at some point, have an issue with the noise your neighbor is making, then you should express that with the following phrases:

Ich muss mit Ihnen sprechen – I need to talk to you.

Gibt es ein Problem? – Is there a problem?

Hatten Sie eine Party letzten Samstag? – Did you have a party last Saturday?

Ja, es war eher eine kleine Party – Yes, it was more of a small party.

Es war schon ziemlich laut – It was really loud.

Das war nicht meine Absicht. Entschuldigen Sie bitte – It was not my intention. I apologize.

Es ist schon in Ordnung, wenn Sie andere zu sich in die Wohnung rufen, aber ich konnte kein bisschen schlafen. Die ganze Nacht hörte ich die Musik und das laute Reden – It is okay if you invite others to the apartment, but I could not sleep for a while. All night I heard the music and loud talking.

Ich entschuldige mich vielmals für den Lärm – I apologize for the noise a lot.

Könnten Sie es nächtes mal ein wenig leiser machen? Das wäre mir sehr Recht – Could you make it a little quieter next time? I would appreciate that.

Ja, sicher. Ich verspreche es! – Yes, sure. I promise it!

Vielen Dank – Thank you very much.

Alles klar. Und ich entschuldige mich nochmals für die Unannehmlichkeiten – All right. And I apologize again for the inconvenience.

And last, but not least, when you want to move out, here are some phrases you could use:

Wie geht's? – How are you doing?

Gut. Was gibt es? – Good, what is up?

Ich muss mit Ihnen über etwas sprechen – I need to talk with you about something.

Klar. Um was geht es? – Sure. What is it about?

Ich wollte Ihnen Bescheid geben, dass ich bald ausziehen möchte – I wanted to let you know that I would like to move out soon.

Wann? – When?

In den nächsten paar Wochen – In the next few weeks.

Das verstehe ichnicht. Warum möchten Sie ausziehen? – I just do not understand why you want to move out?

Ich habe einen Job in einer anderen Stadt bekommen. Deswegen muss ich bald gehen, damit ich mich auch in der anderen Stadt zurechtfinden kann, bevor ich mit dem Job anfange – I got a job in another city. That is why I have to go soon, in order to get to know the city, before I start the job.

Ja, das verstehe ich – Yes, I understand that.

Vielen Dank für Ihr Verständnis. Ich werde Ihnen Bescheid geben, wenn die Zeit gekommen ist – Thank you for your understanding. I will let you know when the time comes.

Alles klar. Das passt – All right. That is good.

We will now go over the **important verbs** from the lesson.

The verb "abbiegen – to turn (right/left)" is very important for describing the way.

We conjugate it like this, in the present:

Ich bieg(e) ab

Du biegst ab

Er biegt ab

Wir biegen ab

Ihr biegt ab

Sie biegen ab

It is a separable verb that has a preposition. We will always conjugate verbs like this by adding the right endings to the verb stem and putting the preposition at the end.

When we put it in a sentence, it will be like this:

Ich biege rechts ab – I turn right.

Du musst links abbiegen – You have to turn left.

Another verb is "vorbeigehen – to go past".

It is the same:

Ich geh(e) vorbei

Du gehst vorbei

Er geht vorbei

Wir geh(e)n vorbei

Ihr geht vorbei

Sie geh(e)n vorbei

Sie gehen an den Park vorbei – They go past the park.

Du musst an der Schule vorbeigehen – You need to go past the school.

Another important part you need to learn is the **SUBJUNCTIVE II**.

You could see its use in some examples in this lesson.

"könnte, würde, hätte...usw".

We will now go over it:

The subjunctive II is used in German to express requests, wishes, unrealistic possibilities, and conjectures. The subjunctive II is formed with the auxiliary verb "würden" (would) and the infinitive at the end of the sentence.

"würden" is conjugated like this:

ich würde

du würdest

er, sie, es würde

wir würden

ihr würdet

sie würden

Würden Sie mir bitte den Zimmerschlüssel geben? – Would you please give me the room key?

Was würden Sie empfehlen? – What would you recommend?

The verbs "haben", "sein", and the modal verbs form the subjunctive with the forms of the preterite and umlaut.

haben

ich hätte

du hättest

er, sie, es hätte

wir hätten

ihr hättet

sie hätten

Ich hätte gerne das Mittagessen im Zimmer – I would like to have the lunch in my room.

sein

ich wäre

du wärst

er, sie, es wäre

wir wären

ihr wäret

sie wären

Ich wäre gerne in Spanien – I would like to be in Spain.

können

ich könnte

du könntest

er, sie, es könnte

wir könnten

ihr könntet

sie könnten

Könntest du mir bitte helfen? – Could you please help me?

müssen

ich müsste

du müsstest

er, sie, es müsste

wir müssten

ihr müsstet

sie, müssten

Ich müsste in die Toilette – I would need to go to the bathroom.

dürfen

ich dürfte

du dürftest

er, sie, es dürfte

wir dürften

ihr dürftet

sie dürften

Dürfte ich das Password für den WLAN haben? – Could I get the password for the Wi-Fi?

sollen

ich sollte

du solltest

er, sie, es sollte

wir sollten

ihr solltet

sie sollten

Sie sollten sich umbedingt die Veranstaltung ansehen – You should go see the event.

With the subjunctive, one can express a wish. Often the particles are used "doch", "bloß" and "nur" (just, only).

Mit dem Konjunktiv kann man einen Wunsch ausdrücken. Oft werden dabei die Partikeln "doch", "bloß", und "nur" benutzt.

Wenn er doch bald kommen würde! – If only he would come soon!

Wenn ich nur Urlaub hätte! – If only I had holidays!

With the subjunctive, one can give advice. For this, you use the modal verb "sollen-should".

Du solltest im Bett liegen – You should lay in bed.

With the subjunctive, one can express something unreal/a possibility.

Wenn du schneller laufen könntest, würden wir den Bus nicht verpassen – If you could run faster, we would not miss the bus.

With the subjunctive, one can express a conjecture.

Es ist zwar noch nicht sehr spät, aber er könnte schon zu Hause sein – It is not very late, but he could be home.

A polite request can be expressed in a sentence with the subjunctive II:

Könnten Sie das Fenster zumachen? – Could you close the window?

Könntest du mir bitte helfen, den Koffer nach oben zu tragen? – Could you please help me to carry the suitcase upstairs?

It is also important for you to learn the **FUTURE I.**

In German, the use of the present with a verb is usually sufficient to express future-oriented actions or intentions.

Wir ziehen in einem Monat nach Berlin um – We are moving to Berlin in one month.

Ich sehe mir morgen den neuen Film an – I am watching the new movie tomorrow.

Future I is a tense that directly describes a situation in the future. It is formed with the auxiliary verb "werden" and the infinitive of the corresponding verb, which must be at the end of the sentence.

Ich werde sehr viel lernen – I will lean a lot.

Ich werde Mario heiraten – I will marry Mario.

Wir werden in einem Hotel bleiben – We will stay in a hotel.

So that is it for this lesson. We will now move on. Are you ready?

Chapter 10 – Common Questions and Phrases Everyone Needs to Know

Now that we have covered the most common and important topics, we will now list some of the most common phrases that are useful in many different situations. You might need to visit the doctor or ask for help if you have an accident. Thus, it is important to know these phrases.

General phrases and expressions for everyday situations:

Sometimes you will just need to answer with a simple "okay", and guess what? Germans say "okay" the same as people do in English.

Okay is just Okay!

Another affirmation is: Natürlich, selbstverständlich, **which means "of course".**

However, you can also emphasize a negation:

Natürlich nicht! – **Of course not!**

When you want to say more than just "okay", you can say:

Das ist okay – **That's fine.**

And some more affirmations are:

Das ist richtig – That is right

Sicher – Sure

Sicherlich – Certainly

Bestimmt; auf jeden Fall – Definitely

Auf jeden Fall – Absolutely

When someone says:

Wann sehen wir uns? – When do we see each other?

You answer:

So bald wie möglich – As soon as possible!

Or:

Ich bin mir nicht sicher. Ich werde dir Bescheid geben – I am not sure. I will let you know.

Das ist genug – That is enough.

When, for example, your friend says:

Sorry, ich konnte nicht zur Party kommen – Sorry, I could not make it to the party.

You can just say:

Das macht nichts – It does not matter.

Ist nicht schlimm – It is not important.

Or, when someone asks you about an issue you have or some problem that you are solving, you can just say:

Es ist nichts Ernstes – It is not serious.

Es ist nicht der Rede wert – It is not worth it.

When you want to tell someone that you do not have time to talk or that you need to go, you can say:

Ich habe es eilig – I am in a hurry.

Ich muss gehen – I have got to go.

Ich gehe aus – I am going out.

Schlaf gut – Sleep well.

If a person says to you:

Schönen Tag wünsche ich! – I wish you a nice day!

You can simply say:

Gleichfalls! – Same to you!

Or if you want to agree with someone, say:

Ich auch – Me too.

When your friend asks you:

Wie war der Film? – How was the movie?

Sometimes you can answer with:

Nicht schlecht – Not bad.

Let's say you are talking about liking someone or something:

Ich mag... – I like...

Ihn – him

Sie – her

Es – it

Or if you do not like someone or something:

Ich mag nicht... – I do not like...

Ihn – him

Sie – her

Es – it

We have already talked about saying "thank you" or "you are welcome", but here are some extended versions that you may need:

Danke für... – Thanks for your...

deine Hilfe – help

deine Gastfreundschaft – hospitality

deine E-Mail – email

Danke für alles – Thanks for everything.

If you need to apologize to someone for something you did or if you just want to show sympathy, you could say:

Es tut mir leid – I am sorry.

Es tut mir wirklich leid – I am really sorry.

Es tut mir leid, dass ich zu spät komme – Sorry I am late.

Es tut mir leid, dich warten zu lassen – Sorry to keep you waiting.

Entschuldige die Verspätung – Sorry for the delay.

When you really want to make someone aware of something, you can say:

Schau! – Look!

Prima! – Great!

Los! – Come on!

War nur ein Witz! – Only joking! (or just kidding!)

Gesundheit! – Bless you! (when someone sneezes)

Das ist lustig! – That is funny!

So ist das Leben! – That is life!

Verdammt! – Damn it!

Sometimes we need to demand or request something. Or, in other words, we need to use the **IMPERATIVE**.

The imperative is used for prompts, commands, advice or clues.

The imperative is built for the following forms:

Du – you

du – for a person

ihr – you

ihr – for two or more people

Sie – you

Sie – as a courtesy for one or more people.

The imperative for the "du-form" is formed without the personal pronoun "du" and the ending "-st".

du kommst → Komm!

du gibst → Gib!

du nimmst → Nimm!

du gehst → Geh!

Geh in die Stadt! – Go to the city!

The imperative for the "ihr-form" is formed without the personal pronoun "ihr".

ihr kommt → Kommt!

ihr gebt → Gebt!

ihr nehmt → Nehmt!

ihr feiert → Feiert!

Kommt schnell her! – Come here quickly!

The imperative for the "Sie-form" is formed by changing the word order.

Sie gehen → Gehen Sie!

Sie geben → Kommen Sie!

Sie kommen → Kommen Sie!

Sie nehmen → Nehmen Sie!

Sie ziehen an → Ziehen Sie an!

Ziehen Sie das Kleid an! – Put on the dress!

Verbs with umlauts in the second and third person singular lose this umlaut in the imperative.

du schläfst → Schlaf!

du fährst → Fahr!

Verbs with the stem-end "-t", "-d", "-ig", "-er", "-el" get the ending "-e" in the "du-form".

du wartest → Warte!

du entschuldigst dich → Entschuldige dich!

du lächelst → Lächle!

Irregular imperative forms

Sein – to be

du → Sei!

ihr → Seid!

Sie → Seien Sie!

Haben – to have

du → Hab!

ihr → Habt!

Sie → Haben Sie!

Werden – to become

du → Werde!

ihr → Werdet!

Sie → Werden Sie!

Imperative – "wir-form"

The imperative for the "we-form" is formed by changing the word order.

wir gehen → Gehen wir!

wir kommen → Kommen wir!

wir geben → Geben wir!

wir nehmen → Nehmen wir!

Now that you know how it is formed, we can move on with some typical phrases in the imperative:

Gehen wir hin! – Let's go there!

Kaufen wir es hier! – Let's buy it here!

Lass uns gehen! – Let's go!

Herein! – Come in!

We can request something in a more polite way:

Nehmen Sie Platz – Please sit down.

Darf ich um Ihre Aufmerksamkeit, bitten? – Could I have your attention, please?

Lass uns gehen! – Let's go!

Beeile dich! – Hurry up!

Mach zu! – Get a move on!

If we want to calm someone down, we can say:

Beruhige dich – Calm down

Bleib' mal ruhig, beruhige dich – Steady on!

Warte mal eine Sekunde – Hang on a second.

Warte mal eine Minute – Hang on a minute.

Einen Moment, bitte – One moment, please.

Einen Augenblick, bitte – Just a minute, please.

Lass dir Zeit – Take your time.

Bitte sei ruhig – Please be quiet.

Halt's Maul! – Shut up!

Hör auf! – Stop it!

Mach dir keine Sorgen – Do not worry.

Vergiss nicht – Do not forget.

Bediene dich selbst – Help yourself.

Mach weiter – Go ahead.

Sag mir bescheid! – Let me know!

If you want to let someone through a door, it is polite to say:

Nach Ihnen! – After you!

When you want to tell someone the location of something:

Wo ist der Stift? – Where is the pen?

Hier – Here

Wo ist das Haus? – Where is the house?

Da, dort – There

Wo finde ich eine Toilette? – Where can I find a toilete?

Überall – Everywhere

Nirgendwo – Nowhere

Irgendwo – Somewhere

Here are some useful questions you could use at some point:

Wo bist du? – Where are you?

Was ist das? (hier) – What is this?

Was ist das? (da) – What is that?

Stimmt etwas nicht? – Is anything wrong?

Was ist los? – What is the matter?

Ist alles in Ordnung? – Is everything okay?

If you want to talk to someone who is busy, then you can say:

Hast du einen Moment Zeit? – Have you got a minute?

Hast du einen Stift, den ich leihen könnte? – Have you got a pen I could borrow?

If you want to be sure about something that someone says, you may ask something like:

Wirklich? – Really?

Bist du sicher? – Are you sure?

Warum? – Why?

Warum nicht? – Why not?

Was ist los? – What is going on?

Was geschieht? – What is happening?

Was ist passiert? – What happened?

Was? – What?

Wo? – Where?

Wann? – When?

Wer? – Who?

Wie? – How?

Wie viele? – How many?

Wie viel? – How much?

Now here are some things you can say when congratulating someone or wishing someone good luck:

Herzlichen Glückwunsch! – Congratulations!

Gut gemacht! – Well done!

Viel Glück! – Good luck!

So ein Pech! – Bad luck!

Macht nichts! – Never mind!

Wie schade! – What a pity! (or what a shame!)

Alles Gute zum Geburtstag! – Happy birthday!

Frohes neues Jahr! – Happy New Year!

Frohe Ostern! – Happy Easter!

Frohe Weihnachten! – Happy Christmas! (or Merry Christmas!)

Frohen Valentinstag – Happy Valentine's Day!

When someone has good news, you can simply say:

Ich bin froh, das zu hören – Glad to hear it.

Or if someone has bad news, then you could say:

Es tut mir leid, das zu hören – Sorry to hear that.

You will also have to express your needs or emotions at some point. When expressing how we feel, we often begin the sentence with "Ich bin" (I am) and add the feeling to it. Let's take a look:

Ich bin müde – I am tired.

Ich bin kaputt – I am exhausted.

Ich bin hungrig – I am hungry.

Ich bin durstig – I am thirsty.

Mir ist langweilig – I am bored.

Ich mache mir Sorgen – I am worried.

Ich freue mich darauf – I am looking forward to it.

Ich habe gute Laune – I am in a good mood.

Ich habe schlechte Laune – I am in a bad mood.

Ich habe keine Lust – I cannot be bothered.

Here are some more options for greetings and saying goodbye:

Willkommen! – Welcome!

If you have a guest who is visiting, you can say:

Willkommen… – Welcome to…

Deutschland – Germany

Lange nicht gesehen! – Long time, no see!

Alles Gute! – All the best!

Bis morgen! – See you tomorrow!

When you want to know someone's opinion or if you want to express yours, you can use the following phrases:

Was meinst du? – What do you think?

Ich finde, dass… – I think that…

Ich hoffe, dass… – I hope that…

Ich fürchte, dass… – I am afraid that…

Meiner Meinung nach… – In my opinion…

Ich bin einverstanden – I agree.

Ich bin nicht einverstanden – I disagree (or I do not agree).

Das ist wahr – That is true.

Das ist nicht wahr – That is not true.

Ich denke es – I think so.

Ich denke nicht – I do not think so.

Ich hoffe es – I hope so.

Ich hoffe nicht – I hope not.

Du hast Recht – You are right.

Du liegst falsch – You are wrong.

Es macht mir nichts aus – I do not mind.

Das hängt von dir ab – It is up to you.

Es kommt darauf an – That depends.

Das ist interessant – That is interesting.

Das ist lustig – That is funny.

When you arrive in Germany, you will probably need to make it clear if you can speak German and how good you are at it. A stranger can ask you, or you might need to ask someone if he or she speaks English. To have a successful conversation, you can use the following phrases:

Sprechen Sie Deutsch? – Do you speak German?

Sprechen Sie Englisch? – Do you speak English?

Ich spreche kein Deutsch/Englisch – I do not speak German/English.

Mein Deutsch ist nicht sehr gut – My German is not very good.

Ich spreche nur ein kleines bisschen Deutsch – I only speak a little German.

Ich spreche ein bisschen Deutsch – I speak a little German.

Können Sie bitte etwas langsamer sprechen? – Could you please talk a little slower?

Können Sie das bitte aufschreiben? – Could you write it down?

Könnten Sie das bitte wiederholen? – Can you please repeat that?

Ich verstehe – I understand.

Ich verstehe nicht – I do not understand.

Other simple phrases:

Ich weiß – I know

Ich weiß nicht – I do not know

Entschuldigen Sie bitte, wo ist die Toilette? – Sorry, where is the toilet please?

Then you will come across some signs that you need to understand in order to find your way:

Eingang – entrance

Ausgang – exit

Notausgang – emergency exit

Drücken – push

Ziehen – pull

Toiletten – toilets

WC – WC

Herren – men/gentlemen

Damen – women/ladies

Frei – free

Besetzt – occupied/reserved

Außer Betrieb – out of order

Rauchen verboten – smoking forbidden

Privat – private

Kein Zutritt – no entry

Sometimes you will need to pass someone somewhere or ask for something politely. Then you can say the following sentences:

Entschuldigen Sie, bitte – Excuse me, please.

Entschuldigung – Sorry.

If someone apologizes to you, you can answer with one of the following expressions:

Kein Problem – No problem.

Das macht nichts or macht nichts – That does not matter (or it does not matter).

Machen Sie sich keine Sorgen – Do not worry.

Emergencies

No matter where you go, you can never predict what is going to happen. We hope for the best, of course, but it is good to know the most important words and phrases when you need help or when you are searching for something or someone and need assistance as soon as possible. To make sure that everything goes fine, here are some phrases that can be very helpful in certain situations:

(Note that in a serious emergency, you can reach emergency services in Germany and 112 connects you to the police.)

When you need immediate help on the spot, you can shout:

Hilfe! – Help!

Or when you need to warn someone:

Seien Sie vorsichtig! – Be careful!

Achtung! – Attention!

Bitte helfen Sie mir – Please help me.

If there are medical emergencies, you can use these phrases:

Rufen Sie einen Krankenwagen! – Call an ambulance!

Ich brauche einen Arzt – I need a doctor.

Es gab einen Unfall – There was an accident.

Bitte beeilen Sie sich! – Please hurry up!

Ich habe mich geschnitten – I have cut myself.

Ich habe mich verbrannt – I have burnt myself.

Ist alles in Ordnung? – Is everything fine?

Geht es allen gut? – Is everyone fine?

Sometimes, especially when visiting another city, there can be thieves that try to rob tourists, or some people can also try to fool you. Therefore, you might need the following phrases:

Haltet den Dieb! – Stop the thief!

Rufen Sie die Polizei! – Call the police!

Mein Geldbeutel wurde gestohlen – My wallet was stolen.

Meine Handtasche wurde gestohlen – My handbag was stolen.

Mein Laptop wurde gestohlen – My laptop was stolen.

Ich möchte einen Diebstahl melden – I want to report a theft.

Mein Auto wurde aufgebrochen – My car was broken into.

Ich bin ausgeraubt worden – I have been robbed.

Ich bin überfallen worden – I have been attacked.

If there is a fire in the apartment or anywhere else, you can say:

Feuer! – Fire!

Rufen Sie die Feuerwehr! – Call the fire department.

Riechen Sie auch Brandgeruch? – Do you also smell something burning?

Da ist ein Feuer – There is a fire

Das Gebäude brennt – The building is on fire.

Other tough situations:

Ich habe mich verlaufen – I am lost.

Wir haben uns verlaufen – We are lost.

Ich kann nicht finden… – I cannot find..

meine Schlüssel – my keys

meinen Reisepass – passport

mein Handy – mobile

Ich habe verloren… – I have lost…

meinen Geldbeutel – wallet/purse

meinen Fotoapparat – camera

Ich habe mich aus ausgesperrt… – I locked myself out of my…

meinem Auto – car

---

meinem Zimmer – room

If someone is bothering you, just say one of the following phrases:

Lassen Sie mich bitte in Ruhe – Leave me alone please.

Geh weg! – Go away!

And this is how you can thank someone for their help:

Vielen Dank für Ihre Hilfe! – Thank you very much for your help.

Ich schätze Ihre Hilfe – I appreciate your help.

Ich bin sehr dankbar für Ihre Hilfe – I am very thankful for your help.

Vielen lieben Dank! – Thank you so much!

In the pharmacy

If you find yourself in a pharmacy, then you will certainly need to know how to say the name of the product that you need. When you arrive, you can greet the worker and ask for one of the following things:

die Apotheke – pharmacy

die Körperpflegemittel – body care products

These are items that you can probably buy in a regular store, or in a drugstore, but you can also find them in a pharmacy.

You can greet the worker and say:

Guten Tag, haben Sie Aftershave? – Good day, do you have aftershave?

das Aftershave – aftershave

And you can use anything instead of the word "aftershave". It depends on the situation and what you need. Here are some common items:

der Kamm – comb

die Haarspülung – conditioner

die Zahnseide – dental floss

das Deodorant – deodorant

die Haarbürste – hairbrush

die Mundspülung – mouthwash

die Nagelfeile – nail file

die Nagelschere – nail scissors

die Slipeinlage – panty liners

das Parfüm – perfume

der Rasierer – razor

die Rasierklinge – razorblade

die Damenbinden – sanitary towels

der Rasierpinsel – shaving brush

die Rasiercreme – shaving cream

der Rasierschaum – shaving foam

das Rasiergel – shaving gel

das Shampoo – shampoo

das Duschgel – shower gel

die Seife – soap

die Tampons – tampons

die Zahnbürste – toothbrush

die Zahncreme – toothpaste

die Pinzette – tweezers

die Watte – cotton wool

You can also buy cosmetics and ask for:

Ich brauche… – I need…

der Eyeliner – eyeliner

der Lidschatten – eyeshadow

das Gesichtspuder – face powder

die Grundierung, Foundation – primer, foundation

die Haarfarbe, Haartönung – hair coloring, hair dye

das Haargel – hair gel

das Haarspray – hair spray

das Haarwachs – hair wax

die Handcreme – hand cream

das Lipgloss – lip gloss

der Lippenstift – lipstick

das Makeup – makeup

die Wimperntusche – mascara

die Feuchtigkeitscreme – moisturizing cream

der Nagellack – nail varnish

der Nagellackentferner – nail varnish remover

And when you need medicine, here is how you ask for it:

Ich brauche… – I need…

das Antiseptikum – antiseptic

das Aspirin – aspirin

das Fußpilzpuder – athlete's foot powder

die Bandagen – bandages

der Hustensaft – cough mixture

die Durchfalltabletten – diarrhoea tablets

die Pille danach – emergency contraception

die Augentropfen – eye drops

die Erste-Hilfe-Ausrüstung – first aid kit

die Tabletten gegen Heuschnupfen – hay fever tablets

die Tabletten gegen Magenverstimmungen – indigestion tablets

das Abführmittel – laxatives

der Lippenbalsam – lip balm (or lip salve)

die Medizin – medicine

das Nikotinpflaster – nicotine patches

die Schmerzmittel – painkillers

das Paracetamol – paracetamol

das Pflaster – plasters

der Schwangerschaftstest – pregnancy testing kit

das Rezept, die Verschreibung – prescription

die Schlaftabletten – sleeping pills

das Thermometer – thermometer

die Hustenpastille – throat lozenges

die Taschentücher – tissues

die Tabletten gegen Reisekrankheit – travel sickness tablets

die Vitamintabletten – vitamin pills

die Babynahrung – baby foods

die Babytücher – baby wipes

die Kondome – condoms

die Kontaktlinsenlösung – contact lens solution

die Wegwerfwindeln – disposable nappies

die Wärmflasche – hot water bottle

die Sicherheitsnadel – safety pins

die Sonnencreme – sun cream

der Sonnenblocker, Sun-Blocker – sun block

When you find yourself in a pharmacy or drugstore, then you can simply ask for anything you need. Here is an example of a conversation between a pharmacist and buyer:

Guten Tag – Good day.

Guten Tag, wie kann ich Ihnen helfen? – Good day, how can I help you?

After the greeting, you can explain the situation or ask for something specific.

Ich habe Sonnenbrand. Meine Haut ist sehr empfindlich. Haben Sie etwas dafür? – I have sunburn. My skin is very sensitive. Do you have something for it?

Natürlich. Ich würde Ihnen eine Crème empfehlen, damit der Sonnenbrand wieder weggeht und, natürlich, einen Sonnenblocker, damit es nicht nochmal passiert – Of course. I would recommend a cream so that the sunburn goes away again and, of course, a sunblock, so it does not happen again.

Klingt gut. Wieviel kostet die Crème? – Sounds good. How much does the cream cost?

Die Crème kostet 10 Euro und der Sonnenblocker 8 Euro – The cream costs 10 Euro and the sunblock 8 Euro.

Aller klar. Dann nehme ich beides. Haben Sie auch etwas für Halsschmerzen? Mein Sohn hat sich diesen Morgen beschwert – Okay. I will take both. Do you have something for a sore throat? My son complained this morning.

Hat er auch Fieber? – Does he have a fever as well?

Nein, das haben wir gleich überprüft. Sein Hals kratzt nur ein bisschen – No, we checked that out right away. His throat just scratches a bit.

Okay, dann würde ich Ihnen einfach Hustenpastillen empfehlen. Falls es aber nicht besser wird, dann würde ich auch einen Hustensaft empfehlen – Okay, then I would just recommend cough drops. But if it does not get better, then I would also recommend a cough syrup.

Okay, ich nehme dann die Pastillen – Okay, I will take the pastilles.

Alles klar. Das macht dann 25 Euro – All right. That makes 25 Euro.

Bitte – Here.

Vielen Dank für Ihren Besuch – Thank you for the visit.

Aufwiedersehen – Goodbye.

Let's take a look at another dialogue:

Hallo – Hello.

Hallo, was kann ich für Sie tun? – Hello, what can I do for you?

Ich brauche Babytücher, Shampoo, und Pflaster, bitte – I need baby towels, shampoo, and plasters, please.

Kommt gleich. Was für ein Shampoo brauchen Sie denn genau? – Coming. What kind of shampoo do you need exactly?

Für normale Haare. Es ist egal welche Marke – For normal hair. It does not matter which brand.

Passt dieses Shampoo? – Does this shampoo work?

Ja, sicher – Yes, sure.

Wir haben heute ein Sonderangebot falls Sie Interesse haben. Die Wimperntusche von L'Oréal kostet heute nur 10 Euro anstatt 18 Euro – We have a special offer today if you are interested. The mascara by L'Oréal costs only 10 Euro today instead of 18 Euro.

Nein, danke. Ich nehme nur die drei Sachen, die ich wollte – No, thanks. I will just take the three items I wanted.

Alles klar. Das macht 20 Euro, bitte – Okay. That makes 20 Euro, please.

Renting a car

Another typical situation you could encounter when going to another country is renting a car. You might be in a situation where you need a car or simply need to go somewhere but cannot use public transport. Here are some useful phrases.

When you arrive at the place where they rent cars, you can greet the worker and use the following expressions:

Guten Tag. Ich bin daran interessiert, ein Auto zu mieten – Good day. I am interested in renting a car.

Gut. Für wie viele Tage? – All right. How many days?

Ich bräuchte es für eine Woche. Wie viel würde das kosten? – I would need it for a week. How much would it cost?

Das kostet 50 Euro pro Tag bei unbegrenzten Meilen – That costs 50 Euro per day with unlimited miles.

Okay, ich verstehe – Okay, I understand.

Was für ein Fahrzeug möchten Sie denn mieten? Möchten Sie manuell oder automatik? – What kind of vehicle do you want to rent? Do you want manual or automatic?

Ich möchte lieber automatik. Was für Autos haben Sie im Angebot? – I would rather take automatic. What kind of cars do you have on offer?

Wir haben fast alle Marken und Modelle. Woran sind Sie am meisten interessiert? – We have almost all brands and models. What are you most interested in?

Ich wäre am Audi A3 interessiert – I would be interested in the Audi A3.

Alles klar. Haben wir – All right. We have that.

Okay. Hat das Fahrzeug eine Klimanlage? – Okay. Does the car have air conditioning?

Natürlich. Das Auto ist mit allem ausgestattet was Sie für eine gute Fahrt brauchen – Of course. The car is equipped with everything you need for a good trip.

Super, dann möchte ich das Auto gerne sehen und danach auch mieten – Great, then I would like to see the car and then rent it.

Sehen Sie es sich in Ruhe an, und wenn Sie sich entschieden haben, dann rufen Sie mich einfach – Take a look at it, and if you have decided, then just call me.

Ich bräuchte Ihren Führerschein, bitte – I would need your driver's license, please.

Ich muss Sie noch errinern, dass Sie das Auto Sie mit vollem Tank zurückbringen müssen – I have to remind you that you have to bring the car back with a full tank.

Okay, das ist in Ordnung – Okay. That is fine.

Und es muss um 12 Uhr am nächsten Montag zurückgebracht werden – And it has to be returned at 12 o'clock next Monday.

Gut. Ich merke es mir – Good. I will remember that.

Noch eine Frage. Soll ich Benzin or Diesel tanken? – Another question. Should I refuel petrol or diesel?

Benzin, bitte – Petrol, please.

Ich werde Ihnen noch einige Details zeigen, bevor Sie losfahren – I will show you some details before you leave.

Hier sind die Lichter und Anzeigen. Stellen Sie sicher, dass die Lichter eingeschaltet bleiben – Here are the lights and indicators. Make sure to leave the lights on.

So öffnen Sie den Benzintank. Wenn etwas schief geht, können Sie einfach die Haube öffnen, um zu überprüfen, ob alles in Ordnung ist oder rufen Sie uns einfach an – This is how you open the petrol tank. If anything goes wrong, you can simply open the hood to check if everything is fine or just call us.

Okay. Vielen Dank. Kann ich gleich losfahren? – Okay. Many thanks. Can I start now?

Ja, natürlich. Gute Fahrt und alles Gute – Yes, of course. Good drive and all the best.

Danke, Ihnen auch. Auf Wiedersehen – Thank you. Wish you the best too. See you.

Driving with the taxi

Another situation where you might need some help is driving via a taxi. You should know that there are people who will try to fool tourists or people who are not very familiar with the pricing. Or you just might need some phrases so you can explain where you need to go.

If you cannot see any taxi, then you can ask someone on the street:

Wo kann ich ein Taxi bekommen? – Do you know where I can get a taxi?

Hätten Sie eine Taxi-Nummer für mich? – Do you have a taxi number?

Ja, die Nummer ist… – Yes, the number is…

If you are calling the taxi, just say:

Ich möchte ein Taxi, bitte – I would like a taxi, please

Ich brauche ein Taxi – I need a taxi.

Leider sind keine Taxis im Moment verfügbar. Rufen Sie später an – Unfortunately, no taxis are available at the moment. Call later.

Wo befinden Sie sich genau. Können Sie mir die Adresse nennen? – Where are you exactly? Can you give me the address?

Ja, ich bin in der Bachstraße, die Bushaltestelle bei dem Hotel (name) – Yes, I am in the Bachstraße, the bus stop at the hotel (name).

Ja, ich bin gleich bei dem Museum in der Rattstraße – Yes, I am right at the museum on Rattstraße.

Alles klar. Das Taxi wird gleich kommen – All right. A taxi will come soon.

Wie lange muss ich warten? – How long do I need to wait?

Ungefähr 10 Minuten. Passt das? – About 10 minutes. Is it okay?

Ja, super – Yes, great.

When you are finally in the taxi, you can greet the driver by simply saying:

Guten Tag – Good day.

The taxi driver might say:

Haben Sie angerufen? – Did you call?

Ja, das habe ich – Yes, I did.

Wohin soll ich fahren? – Where should I drive?

Ich muss zum Hotel… – I need to go to the hotel…

Ich möchte gerne zum Einkaufszentrum – I would like to go to the mall.

Können Sie mich zum Stadtzentrum bringen? – Can you take me to the city center?

Wieviel würde es bis zum Flughafen kosten? – How much would it cost to get to the airport?

Dies würde ungefähr 20 Euro kosten – That would cost about 20 Euro.

Wieviel kostet das? – How much does it cost?

Können Sie bitte bei der Apotheke anhalten? – Can you please stop at the pharmacy?

Schalten Sie bitte das Taximeter an! – Please turn on the meter!

Wie lange brauchen Sie zum Stadtzentrum? – How long do you need to get to the city center?

Können Sie bitte das Fenster öffnen? – Can you please open the window?

Können Sie bitte das Fenser zu machen? – Can you please close the window?

Werden wir bald da sein? – Will we be there soon?

Wieviel macht das? – How much is that?

Das macht 10 Euro – It makes 10 Euro.

Sie können den Rest behalten – You can keep the change.

Kann ich eine Rechnung haben, bitte? – Can I have the receipt, please?

Können Sie mich um 5 Uhr hier wieder abholen, bitte? – Can you pick me up here at 5 o'clock, please?

Können Sie hier auf mich warten. Ich komme gleich – Can you wait here for me? I will be right back.

Passport control and customs

There are, of course, other situations that you need to be prepared for—like the passport control and customs. You will need some phrases to be able to answer serious questions and other such things.

When you arrive at the airport, you might need these phrases:

Darf ich Ihren Reisepass sehen? – Can I see your passport?

Wohin reisen Sie? – Where are you going to?

Warum reisen Sie nach Deutschland? – Why are you coming to Germany?

Wegen eines Bewerbungsgespräches – Because of a job interview.

Ich reise als Tourist – I am going as a tourist.

Ich besuche meine Familie – I am visiting family.

Ich besuche meine Cousine in Berlin – I am visiting my cousin in Berlin.

Wie lange wollen Sie bleiben? – How long do you plan to stay?

Ich möchte eine Woche bleiben – I want to stay one week.

Wo werden Sie wohnen? – Where will you live?

Ich werde bei meiner Tante wohnen – I will live with my aunt.

Sie müssen dieses Einwanderungsformular ausfüllen – You must complete this immigration form.

Sie müssen dies ausfüllen – You need to fill this out.

Schöne Reise! – Nice trip!

Bitte öffnen Sie Ihre Tasche – Please open your bag.

Haben Sie etwas was Sie deklarieren sollten? – Do you have something you need to declare?

Sie müssen Zoll zahlen – You need to pay duty.

Sie müssen sich hinter die gelbe Linie stellen – You need to wait behind the yellow line.

Halten Sie Ihren Reisepass bereit – Prepare your passport.

Services and repairs

If you need something repaired or need help with anything, then you should use the following phrases.

Maybe you need to repair your phone or camera. Whatever it is, you can help yourself:

Wo kann ich mein Handy reparieren? – Where can I repair my phone?

Ich muss meine Armbanduhr reparieren. Kennen Sie jemanden? – I have to fix my watch. Do you know someone?

Meine Kamera ist kaput. Wo kann ich sie reparieren lassen? – My camera is broken. Where can I fix this?

Der Bildschirm meines Handys ist kaputt – The screen of my phone is broken.

Etwas stimmt mit dem Fernseher nicht. Ich kann ihn nicht anschalten – Something is wrong with the TV. I cannot turn it on.

Könnten Sie bitte meinen Laptop reparieren? Ich brauche ihn für meine Arbeit – Can you please fix my laptop? I need it for my work.

Natürlich. Was stimmt nicht mit ihm? – Of course. What is wrong?

Könnten Sie ihn anschalten? – Can you turn it on?

Wieviel wird das kosten? – How much will this cost?

Wie lange brauchen Sie dafür und wann wird er fertig sein? – How long will it take for you and when will it be ready?

Ich kann es gleich reparieren. Ich brauche vielleicht eine Stunde. Passt das? – I can fix it right now. I might need an hour. Is that all right?

Er wird erst morgen fertig sein – It can only be ready tomorrow.

Passt nächste Woche? – Is the next week okay?

Das kann ich nicht in einer Woche schaffen. Ich brauche mindestens zwei Wochen – I cannot do it in a week. I need at least two weeks.

Können Sie es reparieren? – Will you be able to repair it?

Ja, das kann ich – Yes, I can.

Nein, leider kann ich hier nichts mehr tun – No, I unfortunately cannot do anything about it.

Wir müssen es dem Hersteller zurücksenden – We need to send it back to the manufacturer.

Meine Uhr tickt nicht mehr – My watch does not tick anymore.

Kann ich sie mir ansehen? – Can I take a look?

Ja, bitte – Yes, please.

Das Problem ist, dass sie neue Batterien braucht – The problem is that it needs new batteries.

Alles klar – All right.

Ich bin gekommen, um meine Uhr abzuholen. Ist sie fertig? – I came to pick up my watch. Is it ready?

Ja; alles funktioniert jetzt perfekt – Yes, everything works perfectly now.

Wir konnten sie leider nicht reparieren. Sie funktioniert nicht – Unfortunately we could not fix it. It does not work.

If you need someone to print your photos from the vacation, here are some useful phrases:

Können Sie diese Fotos bitte entwickeln? – Can you please print these photos?

Ich möchte diese Fotos drucken lassen, aber bitte matt – I want to print these photos, but please make them matt.

Welche Größe? – What size?

Normale Größe – Regular size.

And if you need your clothes cleaned or fixed, then say:

Könnten Sie dieses Kleid waschen? – Could you clean this dress?

Wieviel kostet das? – How much is it?

Die Hosen sind mir zu lang. Könnten Sie diese etwas kürzen? – The pants are too long for me. Can you cut this a bit?

Ich habe ein Loch in den Hosen. Könnten Sie das flicken? – I have a hole in my pants. Can you fix it?

Ich muss meine Schuhe reparieren lassen. Ich brauche neue Sohlen. Könnten Sie das machen? – I have to fix my shoes. I need new soles. Can you do that?

At the post office

You also may find yourself at the post office or bank. Here are some useful phrases.

When you are at the post office, you will need to speak to the worker in order to pick up something or send an item:

Ich muss diesen Brief verschicken. Was für eine Briefmarke brauche ich? – I have to send this letter. What kind of stamp do I need?

Wieviel kostet die Briefmarke? – How much is the stamp?

Ich brauche einen Umschlag, bitte – I need an envelope, please.

Ich brauche ein Paket Umschläge – I need a package of envelopes.

Wo befindet sich die Post? – Where is the post office?

Ich muss dieses Paket nach Berlin versenden. Wieviel kostet das? – I need to send this package to Berlin. How much will this cost?

Ich muss es wiegen, und dann sage ich es Ihnen – I have to weigh it, and then I will tell you.

Es macht 10 Euro – This will be 10 Euro.

Wo kann ich die Briefmarke kaufen? – Where can I buy the stamp?

Wo kann ich Postkarten kaufen? – Where can I buy postcards?

Was ist im Paket enthalten? – What are the contents of the package?

Es sind Kleider und Socken darin – There are dresses and socks.

In diesem Paket befindet sich ein PC – This package contains a PC.

Wie lange braucht es nach Berlin? – How long does it take to reach Berlin?

Ungefähr drei Tage – Approximately three days.

Bitte verschicken Sie diesen Brief per Einschreiben – Please have this letter sent by registered mail.

Ich möchte diesen Brief mit Nachverfolgungverschicken. Könnten Sie das machen? – I would like to send this letter as a recorded delivery. Can you do that?

Dieses Paket muss als Sonderzustellung geliefert warden, bitte – This package must be delivered as a special delivery, please.

Wo befindet sich hier der Briefkasten? – Where is the mailbox here?

Wann sollte ich das verschicken, damit es auch rechtzeitig zu Weinachten ankommt? – When should I send this so that it arrives in time for Christmas?

Ich möchte ein Paket abholen—Von Mark Müller aus Australien – I would like to pick up a package—from Mark Müller from Australia.

Ich möchte diese Rechnung bezahlen – I want to pay this bill.

Ich möchte Geld nach Deutschland verschicken – I want to send money to Germany.

Verkaufen Sie Postkarten, Geburtstagskarten, Weihnachtskarten? – Do you sell postcards, birthday cards, Christmas cards?

Können Sie bitte dieses Formular ausfüllen? – Can you please fill in this form?

Haben Sie ein Kopiergerät? – Do you have a photocopier?

In the bank

You may at some point go to a bank to open an account or send/receive money. Here is how you should talk with the bankers:

Guten Tag, wie kann ich Ihnen helfen? – Good day, how can I help you?

Guten Tag, ich möchte gerne ein Bankkonto eröffnen – Hello, I would like to open a bank account.

In Ordnung. Was für ein Bankkonto würden Sie denn gerne haben? – All right. What kind of bank account would you like to have?

Ich möchte gerne ein Sparkonto haben – I would like to have a savings account.

Okay. Ich muss Sie daran errinern, dass Sie dafür ein Deposit mit einem Minimum von 50 Euro brauchen – Okay. I must remind you that you need a deposit with a minimum of 50 Euro.

Gut, Ich werde 100 Euro einzahlen. Geht das? – Well, I will deposit 100 Euro. Is that okay?

Natürlich. Warten Sie bitte ein wenig. Ich werde das Konto jetzt einrichten – Of course. Please wait a bit. I will set up the account now.

Alles klar. Vielen Dank – All right. Thank you.

Another situation that you can encounter is when you want to withdraw money. These phrases will help:

Guten Tag. Ich möchte Geld abheben – Good day. I would like to withdraw money.

In Ordnung. Wieviel möchten Sie gern abheben? – All right. How much would you like to withdraw?

Ich möchte gerne 150 Euro abheben – I would like to withdraw 150 Euro.

Haben Sie eine Karte oder Bankkonto? – Do you have a card or bank account?

Ich möchte es von meinem Sparkonto abheben, bitte – I would like to withdraw it from my savings account, please.

Alles klar. Einen moment, bitte – All right. One moment, please.

Können Sie mir Ihren Ausweis geben, bitte? – Could you give me your ID, please?

Ja, hier – Yes, here.

Okay, unterschreiben Sie bitte hier noch – Okay, please sign here.

Vielen Dank – Thank you very much.

Kann ich noch etwas für Sie tun oder ist das alles? – Can I still do something for you, or is that all?

Das ist alles. Danke – That is all. Thank you.

Also, when you need to transfer some money, you can use the following phrases:

Guten Tag. Wie kann ich Ihnen helfen? – Good day. How can I help you?

Guten Tag. Ich würde gerne Geld überweisen – Good day. I would like to transfer money.

In Ordnung. Von woher möchten Sie das Geld denn überweisen? – All right. From where do you want to transfer the money?

Ich möchte es von meinem Sparkonto machen – I want to do it from my savings account.

Gut, Wem möchten Sie das Geld zukommen lassen? – Well, who would you like to send the money to?

Ich möchte es an einen Freund in Berlin überweisen – I would like to send it to a friend in Berlin.

Können Sie mir das Bankkonto geben? – Could you give me the bank account?

Wieviel möchten Sie überweisen? – How much would you like to transfer?

Ich möchte 300 Euro überweisen – I would like to transfer 300 Euro.

Alles klar. Wird gemacht – All right. It is being done.

Ist das alles? – Is that all?

Ja, das ist alles. Vielen Dank – Yes, that is all. Thank you very much.

If you need to cancel an account, this is how you should do it:

Guten Tag. Ich möchte mein Konto schließen, bitte – Good day. I want to close my account, please.

Guten Tag. Gibt es den ein Problem mit dem Konto? – Good day. Is there a problem with the account?

Nein, ich brauche das Konto einfach nicht mehr – No, I just do not need the account anymore.

In Ordnung. Was möchten Sie mit dem Geld auf dem Konto machen? – All right. What do you want to do with the money in the account?

Sie können es auf mein Sparkonto überweisen. Ist das so okay? – You can transfer it to my savings account. Is that okay?

Ja, das mache ich – Yes, I will do that.

Super. Vielen Dank – Great. Thanks.

Möchten Sie vielleicht noch Geld abheben? – Do you maybe want to withdraw money?

Nein, jetzt nicht – No, not for now.

Okay. Bitte warten Sie ein paar Minuten bis ich das Konto schließe. Dann wird das Geld auf das Sparkonto überwiesen, und Sie können es von dort aus abheben, wenn nötig. Falls Sie Interesse an anderen Angeboten haben, können Sie mich gerne fragen. Ich werde Ihnen dann alles erklären – Okay. Please wait a few minutes until I close the account. Then the money is transferred to the savings account, and you can withdraw it from there, if necessary. If you are interested in other offers, you can ask me. I will explain everything.

Okay, ich werde warten. Nein, danke. Ich brauche erstmal nichts –
Okay, I will wait. No thanks. I do not need anything now.

If you want to cash a check, then you can use these phrases:

Hallo, was kann ich für Sie tun? – Hello, what can I do for you?

Ich möchte eine Einzahlung tätigen – I want to make a deposit.

Okay. Soll es ein Scheck oder Bargeld sein? – Okay. Should it be a
check or cash?

Ich möchte einen Scheck einzahlen, bitte – I would like to deposit a
check, please.

Können sie diesen bitte unterschreiben? – Can you please sign this?

Ja, natürlich – Yes, of course.

Möchten Sie etwas Geld zurückhaben? – Would you like to have
some money back?

Ja, bitte – Yes, please.

Wieviel möchten Sie denn? – How much do you want?

Ich möchte gerne 200 Euro haben – I would like 200 Euro.

Hier, bitte – Here.

Vielen Dank dafür – Thank you very much for it.

If you are at a shop or paying with a card, and it gets declined, you
could use these phrases:

Das alles macht 30 Euro, bitte – It comes to 30 Euro, please.

Hier, Sie können es von der Karte nehmen – Here, you can put it on
the card.

Bitte geben Sie den Code ein – Please put in the code.

Alles klar – All right.

Da ist aber ein Problem mit der Karte – There is a problem with the
card.

Was für ein Problem? – What kind of problem?

Sie wurde gerade abgelehnt – It was declined.

Wie das denn? Das ist nicht möglich – How is that? That is not possible.

Haben Sie vielleicht eine andere Karte oder Bargeld? – Do you have another card or cash?

Nein, ich habe nur diese Karte, und Bargeld habe ich nicht – No, I only have this card, and I do not have cash.

Es tut mir wirklich leid, aber diese Artikel können Sie nicht mitnehmen – I am really sorry, but you cannot take these items with you.

Ja, ich verstehe. Ich komme morgen wieder – Yes, I understand. I will come back tomorrow.

Let's say you go into a bank and you want to ask about their fees:

Ist das alles? – Is that everything?

Ich habe eine Frage. Ich interessiere mich für die Gebühren – I have a question. I am interested in the fees.

Was für Gebühren? – What fees?

Mich interessieren die Überziehungsgebühren. Wie hoch sind diese denn? – I am interested in the overdraft fees. How big are these?

Bei jeder Überziehung müssen Sie eine Gebühr zahlen – Every time you overdraft, you will have to pay a fee.

Wie hoch sind diese? – How high is the fee?

Bei jede Überziehung, warden 15 Euro fällig – For every overdraft, you have to pay 15 Euro.

Das ist aber wirklich viel. Meinen Sie nicht auch? – That is really a lot. Don't you agree?

Es soll das Überziehen verhindern – It should prevent the overdraft.

Ja, vielleicht, aber das wird es wahrscheinlich nicht. Es ist einfach zu viel – Yes, maybe, but it probably will not. It is just too much.

Es tut mir leid. Kann ich Ihnen mit etwas anderem helfen? – I am so sorry. Can I help you with something else?

Für heute wäre das alles – That would be everything for today.

If you did not get a bank statement, then you could use the following expressions:

Hallo, was kann ich für Sie tun? – Hello, what can I do for you?

Ich habe ein Problem – I have an issue.

Was für ein Problem? – What kind of issue?

Ich habe erfahren, dass ich irgendwelche Schulden habe. Doch ich habe nie einen Kontoauszug bekommen – I have learned that I have some debts. But I never got a bank statement.

Das tut mir leid. Ich werde nachsehen – I am sorry. I will look it up.

Die Schulden die ich jetzt zahlen muss sind viel größer, und ich wusste das nicht mal – The debts I have to pay now are much bigger, and I did not even know that.

Ich entschuldige mich vielmals. Ich sehe was Sie meinen – I apologize many times. I see what you mean.

Okay, was machen Sie jetzt? Wie lösen wir das Problem? – Okay, what will you do now? How do we solve the problem?

Machen Sie sich keine Sorgen. Ich werde Ihre geschuldeten Gebühren stornieren – Do not worry. I will cancel your due fees.

Heißt das, dass ich nichts zahlen muss? – Does that mean I do not have to pay anything?

Sie werden nur die Anfangsgebühr zahlen müssen. Ist das in Ordnung? – You will only have to pay the initial fee. Is it okay?

Das passt so. Vielen Dank für Ihre Hilfe – That is okay. Many thanks for your help.

Talking to the cabin crew and passengers

There are many other situations you might encounter when traveling and visiting a new city. However, you also need to be aware that you may have to talk to the cabin crew on your flight. Maybe you need some additional information or just want to start practicing your skills on the way to your destination. This is a great opportunity. Let's look at some phrases.

You might want to talk to the flight attendant:

Entschuldigen Sie, bitte. Ich habe einige Fragen – Excuse me, please. I have some questions.

Gerne, fragen Sie – Gladly, just ask.

Ich habe die Anweisungen während des Fluges überhört. Können Sie mir einige Fragen beantworten? – I overheard the instructions during the flight. Can you answer a few questions?

Ja, natürlich. Ich würde sehr gerne helfen und alles wieder für Sie wiederholen, wenn nötig. Fragen Sie doch einfach – Yes, of course. I would love to help and repeat everything for you again if necessary. Just ask.

Okay. Wo befindet sich denn der nächste Ausgang? – Okay. Where is the closest exit?

Sie haben neben dem Sitz eine Karte. Diese zeigt Ihnen wo der nächste Ausgang ist. In diesem Fall befindet sich Ihr nächster Ausgang gleich neben Ihnen, wie Sie sehen können – You have a card next to the seat. This will show you where the closest exit is. In this case, your closest exit is next to you, as you can see.

Alles klar. Wo befindet sich die Toilette? – All right. Where is the toilet?

Die Toilette befindet sich vor Ihnen. Sehen Sie das Schild dort drüben? Das ist die Toilette – The toilet is in front of you. Do you see the sign over there? That is the toilet.

Was wenn etwas passiert? Wenn das Flugzeug ins Wasser abstürzt? Was mache ich dann? – What if something happens? When the plane crashes into the water? What do I do then?

Machen Sie sich keine Sorgen. Die Rettungsjacken sind unter Ihrem Sitz. Es gibt auch Rettungsboote – Do not worry. The jackets are under your seat. There is also a dropship.

Wie bleibe ich sicher? Was kann ich tun, damit mir nichts passiert? – How do I stay safe? What should I do so that nothing happens to me?

Sie sollen einfach ruhig bleiben. Öffnen Sie auf keinen Fall den Gurt. Nur wenn der Pilot es sagt, dann machen Sie es. Aber alles ist in Ordnung, und Sie können Ihren Flug genießen – You should just stay calm. Never open the belt. Only if the captain says so, then do it. But everything is fine, and you can enjoy the flight.

Talking to another passenger

You can also start a conversation with a fellow passenger if you see that he or she is willing to talk:

Heute schneit es aber richtig, oder? – It is snowing hard today, isn't it?

Ja, das Wetter spielt wieder mal verrückt, gerade wenn man mit dem Flugzeug reisen muss – Yes, the weather is crazy again, just when one has to travel by plane.

Genau. Ehrlich gesagt bin ich auch sehr nervös bei solchem Wetter. Ich mag es nicht zu reisen, wenn es draußen schlecht ist – Exactly. Honestly, I am very nervous in such weather. I do not like to travel when it is like this outside.

Ich glaube dass sich niemand dabei wohl fühlt. Aber das passiert halt. Man muss einfach gelassen bleiben – I believe that nobody feels comfortable with it. But that happens. You just have to relax.

Was meinen Sie, wird es so den ganzen Flug über sein? – What do you think, will it be like this the whole flight?

In den Nachrichten habe ich gesehen, dass der Sturm für eine Weile da sein wird – I have seen in the news that the storm will be there for a while.

Ich mache mir echt Sorgen. Es sieht schlimm aus. Ich hoffe, dass alles gut geht – I am really worried. It looks bad. I hope everything goes well.

Der Pilot weiß, was er tut. Das ist nicht das erste Mal, dass er bei solchem Wetter fliegt. Sie sollten sich wirklich keine Sorgen machen – The pilot knows what he is doing. This is not the first time he has been flying in such weather. You really should not worry.

Wird er uns Bescheid geben, wenn etwas schief läuft? Wann sollen wir uns anschnallen? – Will he let us know if something goes wrong? When should we fasten the seatbelts?

Er wird es uns schon sagen, wenn er der Meinung ist, dass wir das tun sollten – He will tell us if he thinks we should do that.

Meinen Sie, dass wir abstürzen könnten? Entschuldigen Sie, aber ich bin ein wenig ängstlich – Do you think we can crash? Excuse me, but I am a little scared.

Man weiß nie. Aber Sie sollten sich wirklich einfach entspannen. Die Zeit wirdso schneller für Sie vergehen – You never know. But you really should just relax. Time will go by faster like that.

Ordering food and drinks on the flight

When you want to order food or drinks on the flight, you can use these phrases:

Entschuldigung, ich habe mich gefragt, ob ich etwas zu trinken bestellen könnte? – Sorry, I was wondering if I could order something to drink?

Ja, natürlich. Was möchten Sie gerne haben? – Yes, of course. What would you like to have?

Was haben Sie denn alles? – What do you have?

Wir haben Kaffee, Tee, Wasser, alkoholische Getränke, geprässte Säfte, und vieles mehr – We have coffee, tea, soda, alcoholic drinks, squeezed juices, and much more.

Und wieviel kosten die Getränke? – And how much do the drinks cost?

Die alkoholischen Getränke liegen bei 4 Euro, und bei den anderen variieren die Preise. Was interessiert Sie denn? – The alcoholic drinks are 4 Euro, and others vary in price. What interests you?

Wieviel kostet denn eine Limonade? – How much is a lemonade?

Eine Limonade kostet 5 Euro – A lemonade is 5 Euro.

Ich nehme dann die Limonade, aber ohne Zucker, und mit Eis, bitte. Wann wird das Mittagessen serviert? – I will take the lemonade, but without sugar, and ice, please. When will lunch be served?

Sie bekommen einen Snack zum Getränk. Das Mittagessen wird in einer Stunde serviert – You get a snack with the drink. Lunch will be served in an hour.

Okay. Was wird den serviert? – Okay. What is being served?

Ich werde das Menü in zehn Minuten bringen. Sie werden zwischen drei Fleischsorten und fünf Beilagen wählen können. Sie werden es sich selbst ansehen können – I will bring the menu in ten minutes. You will be able to choose between three types of meat and five side dishes. You will be able to see for yourself.

Ja, aber das Problem ist, dass ich Vegetarier bin. Haben Sie auch etwas für mich? – Yes, but the problem is that I am a vegetarian. Do you have something for me?

Es tut mir leid, aber das hätten Sie 3 Tage vor dem Flug anfragen müssen. So wird es schon immer gemacht. Doch ich bin mir sicher, dass es extra Gemüse gibt, welches wir Ihnen servieren können. Passt das? – I am sorry, but you should have asked that 3 days before the flight. That is always how it is done. But I am sure there are extra vegetables that we can serve you. Does that suit you?

Das wusste ich aber nicht. Schade. Ich würde mich freuen, wenn es wenigstens mit dem Gemüse klappt – I did not know that. Too bad. I would be happy if I could at least get the vegetables.

Machen Sie sich keine Sorgen. Ich werde für Sie nachschauen. Wir haben aber immer reichlich Obst und Smoothies, falls Sie Interesse haben? – Do not worry. I will look for you. But we always have plenty of fruit and smoothies, if you are interested?

Ja, das wäre super. Sie können mir es nach dem Mittagessen bringen, bitte. Vielen Dank für Ihre Hilfe – Yes, that would be great. You can bring it to me after lunch, please. Many thanks for your help.

Losing your belongings at the airport or after arriving

Sometimes you might lose your purse or passport at the airport, or you realize it when you land in another city or country. You could use these phrases to help.

You can talk to the stewardess or someone from the cabin crew:

Entschuldigen Sie bitte, ich bräutche Ihre Hilfe. Ich kann meine Tasche nicht finden – Excuse me, I need help. I cannot find my bag.

Was war denn alles in der Tasche? – What was in the bag?

Da war meine Brieftasche, und mein Reisepass – There was my wallet, and my passport.

Wieviel Geld war darin? – How much money was inside?

Ich hatte 300 Euro in der Brieftasche – I had 300 Euro in my wallet.

Okay, hatten Sie Kreditkarten dabei? – Okay, did you have cards there?

Ja, eine Visa Card hatte ich – Yes, a visa card.

Wir können die Notrufnummer wählen und sehen was machbar ist – We can dial the emergency number and see what is possible.

Und was machen wir mit dem Reisepass? – And what do we do about the passport?

Wir müssen in die Botschaft, um es zu melden. Kommen Sie mit mir – We have to go to the embassy to report it. Come with me.

What to be cautious about during your trip

Another situation where you might need some help is when you finally arrive at the destination. You will, of course, enjoy the trip, but you still need to be cautious.

When you arrive in a big city, you can ask the tour guide or someone you think you can trust:

Hey, ich wollte mal fragen, ob Sie mir noch irgendwelche Tipps geben können. Sollte ich auf etwas Bestimmtes aufpassen? – Hey, I wanted to ask if you can give me any tips. Should I be wary of something specific?

Sie sollten schon ein wenig vorsichtig sein. Dies ist der ärmere Teil der Stadt, wo es schon zu Diebstählen kommen kann – You should be a little careful. This is the poorer part of the city, where there can be theft.

Auf was soll ich besonders aufpassen? – What should I pay particular attention to?

Wenn Sie sich in einer größeren Masse von Menschen befinden, dann sollten Sie auf jeden Fall aufpassen. Die Diebe wissen, dass Touristen oft nicht so aufmerksam sind und gerade sie werden zum Opfer – If you are in a greater mass of people, then you should definitely take care. The thieves know that tourists are often not so attentive and they are the victims.

Ich sehe auch, dass es viele Kinder auf den Straßen gibt, die nach Geld fragen – I also see that there are many kids on the streets asking for money.

Es ist besser, dass Sie mit denen und anderen die nach Geld fragen einfach nicht sprechen oder ihnen zu nahe kommen. Sie können einen schnell betrügen und auch berauben. Das passiert oft – It is better that you do not talk or get too close to those and others who ask for money. They can easily cheat and rob you. That happens often.

Sollte ich sonst noch auf etwas aufpassen? – Should I look out for something else?

Falls Sie mal ein Taxi nehmen, dann sollten Sie auf jeden Fall nachschauen, ob der Fahrer den Taximeter einschaltet. Touristen werden oft abgezockt – If you take a taxi, then you should definitely see if the driver turns on the meter. Tourists are often ripped off.

Und was ist mit dem Nachtleben? Sollte ich da auch aufpassen? – And what about the nightlife? Should I be careful?

Nehmen Sie einfach ein Taxi zum Club und wieder zurück. Man weiß nie, wer nachts noch spät herumläuft – Just take a taxi to the club and back again. You never know who walks around late at night.

And now we come to the end of the book! Everything you have read has included useful phrases for several situations. Of course, there are always more phrases and different possibilities to express your needs, but for now, you are all set. From here, take your time and practice, practice, practice!

Conclusion

Congratulations on making it through to the end of this book. We learned a lot together and broadened our knowledge via various topics. You were able to learn the most important verbs, adjectives, and the word order of a sentence, so you can now form sentences that will get you out of any situation when visiting Germany. Make sure to practice the declination, be creative, and form your sentences with other verbs, adjectives, and nouns.

You can now enjoy the learning process and become an excellent speaker. Don't forget to share it with your friends—tell them about your success and leave them speechless! What matters, in the end, is that you can only learn and improve a language when you actively speak and integrate with others—a friend, a family member or a stranger on the street. Whoever it is, dare to talk to the person in German.

This book will always be a guide for you. Go over the topics or just jump to a particular topic one whenever you feel the need.

Finally, if you found this book useful in any way, a review on Amazon is always appreciated!

www.ingramcontent.com/pod-product-compliance
Lightning Source LLC
LaVergne TN
LVHW091214080426
835509LV00009B/990